My Life In Horror
Volume I

by

Kit Power

Cover design and interior layout © WHITEspace, 2020
www.white-space.uk

The moral rights of the author have been asserted in accordance with the Copyright, Designs and Patents Act, 1988.

All rights reserved. No part of this publication may be reproduced or transmitted in any form or by any means, electronic or mechanical, including photocopy, recording, or any information storage and retrieval system, without permission in writing from the publisher.

978-1-912578-98-6

PRAISE FOR *MY LIFE IN HORROR*

"Kit Power is an astonishingly perceptive, enthusiastic and articulate horror critic whose work is as courageously self-aware as it is welcoming."
—Alasdair Stewart, Host: PseudoPod, Hostus Mostus: The Full Lid (BFS and Hugo award finalist)

"A delight and loads of fun, My Life In Horror speaks to the young horror fan in all of us, and goes a long way to explaining why our love of genre is a lifelong affair"
—John Llewellyn Probert, Author and critic.

"Kit Power's enthusiasm for his wide-ranging subjects is infectious, he has an enviable memory, and he captures magnificently the joy and rage of adolescence."
—Tim Major, Author: Snakeskins

"Kit Power is a punk rocker, and My Life In Horror Volume I sees him spitting bile at society and celebrating the underdog in a collection of hugely entertaining essays."
—JR Park, Author: Mad Dog

"Kit Power's My Life In Horror is bursting with passion and near-obsessive insight."
—Chris Hall, DLS Reviews

"Kit Power's journey into the heart of Horror isn't Charles Marlow travelling up the Congo, it's a journey into the very essence of the genre itself. This is a must have book for anyone interested in what makes its servants tick"

—Johnny Mains, Editor

"You'll find a seemingly diverse range of topics here, but at the heart of it all is horror, and there's a lot of heart. Kit Power shows you his on every intimate page. I loved it."

—Ray Cluley, Author: Probably Monsters

"Heartfelt, funny, incisive, and at times profoundly moving, My Life In Horror shows why the genre, and by extension the Arts in general, are so important to our lives."

—Neil Snowdon, Editor: Electric Dreamhouse Press

DEDICATION

Clearly, obviously for Jim, without whom. etc. But also for **Stephen Volk** and **Brian Keene**, two titans of horror whose recent non-fiction tomes *(Coffinmaker's Blues* for Volk, *End Of The Road* for Keene) discuss the reality of being a writer with a level of excoriating honesty that serves as an example to us all. I hope this book lives up to that shining legacy; but either way, you have both been extraordinarily generous with your time and support for this rookie writer, and I am enormously grateful for both. Thank you.

SPECIAL THANKS

The production of this book was funded via a crowdfunding campaign, and you would not be reading it now without the extraordinary generosity of the following people:

RJ Barker (www.rjbarker.co.uk)
Stephen Lindsay Satterfield
Josh Bernhard
Gina Collia
Dave Watkins
Chris Hall of DLS Reviews (www.dlsreviews.com)
Graig, Meadow, and Lorelei Summerland
Antonietta Della Pietra
Gavin Cox
James Everington
Joseph Daniels
David J. Court
Paul Giffney
Robin Ince
Horrific Tales Publishing (www.horrifictales.co.uk)
Jim Mcleod (www.gingernutsofhorror.com)
Rowan B. Fortune (www.rowantree-editing.uk)
Dion Winton-Polak (www.thefinetoothed.com)
Richard Sheehan (www.richardmsheehan.co.uk)
C.A. Yates
Jeremy Nelson
Jonathan James
Patrick R McDonough
Laura Mauro
Michael Green
Rob Hart
David Baume
Robert Gamble
John Sawyer

TABLE OF CONTENTS

Foreword by Jim Mcleod — 13

THE HOLY TRINITY

The Book That Made Me — 21
(IT)

The Film That Made Me — 27
(RoboCop)

The Album That Made Me — 42
(Appetite for Destruction)

PRIMARY YEARS
0 – 11

Minds Immeasurably Superior To Ours — 55
(Jeff Wayne's War of the Worlds)

Alive, But Like A Nightmare — 67
(Indiana Jones and the Temple of Doom)

Feed the World — 76

Sickness Will Surely Take The Mind — 84
(Tommy)

It Is Your Favourite Planet, After All — 92
(Doctor Who and the Terror of the Autons)

Someday, You May Be Ready *(Gremlins)*	101
Old Man, Why Do You Smoke? *(Scott [Absent Friends 1])*	107
Now It's Time To Show You What I Already Know *(The Thing)*	126
A Tanked Up Mob *(Hillsborough)*	133
This Monster That We Call The Earth Is Bleeding *(The Headless Children)*	147
My Brief Career As An Eleven-Year-Old Slave Trader	158

—

SECONDARY YEARS
12 – 16

Assume An Attitude *(Bring Your Daughter to the Slaughter)*	173
Kill Your Brother, You'll Feel Better *(The Lost Boys)*	182
Show Yourself, Destroy Our Fears, Release Your Mask *(Queen: Greatest Hits II)*	194

It's Just A Phase I Was Going Through   212
   (The Wasp Factory)

We Have Such Sights to Show You   220
   (Hellraiser)

Leftovers To Be   230
   (Parents)

You Look Like A Clown In That Stupid Jacket   235
   (Wild at Heart)

—

ALLEGED ADULTHOOD 16+

Of Wolf And Man   245
   (Werewolf: The Apocalypse)

Keep It Up Son, Take A Look At What You Could Have Won   252
   (Endless, Nameless)

Give Me A Chance To Apologise, Okay?   262
   (Sleepers)

Why Don't You Lie Back And Enjoy Being Inferior?   273
   (Last House on the Left)

Our Life In Horror   279
   (Eagles of Death Metal / Queen at Hyde Park)

—

SETTING THE RECORD STRAIGHT: CLARIFICATIONS

Write What Scares You *(On Writing)*	289
Hey, Fuckers! *(Live: F@*k Like a Suicide)*	295
I Happen To Be Crazy. Not Stupid. *(A Death in the Family)*	303
What Have We Learned? *(An Afterword)*	312

FOREWORD
by Jim Mcleod

When it comes to any duration longer than a day, I have no grasp of time's passage. As *Gingernuts of Horror* enters its eleventh (or tenth) year, it fills my heart, mind and soul with joy and elation seeing Kit Power's *My Life in Horror* make the transition from a monthly column on the website, to a fully fledged and expanded print edition.

It is always the case when an author receives any small amount of success or recognition, that everyone says, 'Congratulations, you deserved it'—it has become the standard reply, whether heartfelt or just an insincere platitude, so that you don't appear jealous. However, in Kit's case it is more than deserved; if there is a person working in the genre today who is filled with more passion, love or desire to see it lift itself from the shackles of being the Black Sheep of genre writing, I haven't met them. Kit is a force of nature, a hugely talented writer of both fiction and nonfiction. You can pick up anything that he has written safe in the knowledge that what you will read will be stunning. But my love for Kit transcends his writing; to me he is much more than just a writer.

There is family, and friends, and then there are friends who become family. Kit is like my younger but way more intelligent and enlightened brother. In the however many years (I told you I don't get timescales, and yes it's embarrassing not to know) I have known Kit, he has undoubtedly made my life infinitely better by being a part of it. He has been at my side, keeping me on the straight and narrow for more years than I can remember. He has helped me grow as a person; I am more open, forgiving and accepting just by having him in my life. He has been there as a shoulder to lean on, an ear to talk to and, when needed, has never shied from telling me I have acted a fool, and that I need to put my big boy pants on and make things right. If you have ever spent any amount of time in Kit's company, you will know what I mean. His enthusiasm for the genre and the success of others is so infectious the World Health Organisation has classified Kit as a category HG4 risk.

Like all great friendships, we almost never connected; if I remember correctly, Kit sent in a review request for his first book, and I cannot remember if I just deleted it or gave him one of my standard replies. This was when the site was still a one-person outfit, and if I became overwhelmed, I would unceremoniously dump emails. But that didn't put Kit off; I'm not sure if there is anything that would ever put him off. Later, he sent in a completed '5 Minutes with' interview which would ultimately be the prototype essay on Stephen King's *IT*, and would become the prototype for his *My Life in Horror* article series on the site. Even then I could tell I was onto something special, and to be honest, I was just as much in awe at his eloquence and passion for the book, as I was jealous of his gift for writing engaging and profound articles. But it was his hilarious love letter to *RoboCop*, and his conviction that it is the best film ever made, that sealed the deal.

We then pitched the idea for this to become a monthly column, which turned out to be one of the best decisions I made for the site. In June of 2014, the first official *My Life in Horror* column was born.

Six years later, and here we are all holding a copy of the first volume of his collected essays; I can say with hand on heart that it has been a journey I could live a thousand times over. His articles have never been anything but brilliant, and have resulted in fantastic, once in a lifetime opportunities for both Kit and myself. I would never have been given a chance to interview Joe Dante had it not been for Kit's essay on *Gremlins*, which is still the most shared article to appear on the site with over 5000 shares on Facebook alone. Similarly, we would never have interviewed Ginger from The Wildhearts, a hero to both of us. As for Kit's highs from writing *My Life in Horror*, he has stated that his book on Tommy would never have happened if Neil Snowden (who curates the Midnight Movie Monographs for PS Publishing) had not read his articles on the site. Just knowing that *Gingernuts of Horror* allowed such a thing fills me with so much pride and warm cuddly feelings, I run the risk of losing my reputation as fearsome— 'passionate about the genre, but clearly unwilling to suffer fools gladly, or really at all,' as Kit initially said about me. Seriously, I don't where I get this reputation; I am a big softie, once you get to know me.

If you are holding a copy of this book, having never read Kit's articles, then buckle up and put aside enough time to read it in one sitting. You are holding one of the most exceptional series of collected articles on horror, life, media and the birth of one the most exciting authors to emerge on the scene in recent years.

Here's to you Kit, *Slàinte maith, h-uile latha, na chi 'snach fhaic!, thank you for helping me to become the man I wanna be.*

My Life In Horror

Every month, I write about a film, album, book or event that I consider horror, and that had a warping effect on my young mind. You will discover my definition of what constitutes horror is both eclectic and elastic. Also, of necessity, much of this will be bullshit—that is, my best recollection of things that happened anywhere from fifteen to forty years ago. Sometimes I will revisit the source material contemporaneously, further compounding the potential bullshit factor. Finally, intimate familiarity with the text is assumed—to put it bluntly, here be gigantic and comprehensive spoilers. Though in the vast majority of cases, I'd recommend doing yourself a favour and checking out the original material first anyway.

This is not history. This is not journalism. This is not a review.

This is my life in horror.

THE
HOLY
TRINITY

Author's note: the first three articles were written as my audition pieces for Gingernuts of Horror, *though I did not know that when I wrote them. The Book That Made Me was an ongoing series (later rebranded as Books That Matter, still running on the site). I pitched the piece on RoboCop for a mooted The Film That Made Me spin off, which Jim agreed to publish (again, later rebranded as Films That Matter, and also ongoing). The Album That Made Me proved a bridge too far, alas, though the site does now also provide periodic coverage of Rock and Metal under its 'The Devil's Music' section. Had there been a master plan, I would have likely saved all three of these articles to be huge set pieces as* My Life In Horror *developed, and almost certainly they would have been longer (indeed, for this volume, they are). That said, I kind of dig the all-guns-blazing approach these essays represent—going where the passion was, and letting it all hang out—and hey, they got me the gig, without which you wouldn't be reading this book. Enjoy.*

THE BOOK THAT MADE ME

IT

The first thing you need to know is that I was eleven the first time I read *IT*. There are several implications that flow from that statement, the first and most pressing being a pretty serious meditation on what my parents were thinking, which is a theme this book will return to with some frequency.

I'm sure my mum didn't have a clue what lay between the pages of the lurid red slipcase on the hardback book we'd gotten for 25p from the book club offer on the back of the *Radio Times*. My guess is that she was just happy to see me reading, and that the doorstop-sized tome meant it would take me a while to finish—unlike the Doctor Who target paperbacks I usually devoured over a weekend. My dad, however… My dad had read *IT*, so what can *his* excuse have been?

I could just ask, but it's far more fun to speculate.

I think his reasoning was that I could handle *IT*, and that if I couldn't, I'd just stop reading. In this, he was right and wrong, but I will be forever grateful that he trusted my far-reaching instincts, even as I doubt my capacity to do the same with my own children.

Thanks, Dad.

Because *IT* just blew the fucking doors off.

For starters—and I can say this with a confidence

few others can match—King *nails* the experience of being a child in this book. I couldn't just see the Losers Club; I *knew* them. By the time we'd been properly introduced, and gone down the smoke hole to have a vision, I *was* one of them, breathing in the thick acrid fumes, trying not to cough, willing the visions to come.

I laughed with those kids, and I got sad when they did, and I hated their bullies; even as Mr. King took me inside their minds, showed me how damaged they were, how their meanness was a byproduct of neglect and parental indifference or hostility. *IT* showed me not the trite old bullshit thing about bullies being cowards (how, exactly, does that help when you're the shortest kid in class?), but rather that bullies are *broken*, malformed by circumstance and shitty role-modelling, human animals reacting as animals do to pain.

Showed is the key word. *IT* is a big book, a long book, and one of the many advantages that gives is that Mr. King never has to tell us anything—he can just *show it*. And he does, time and time again—he sees, he shows, he does not judge. There is a lot of death; specifically, there's a lot of child death. We witness it often, and it is unflinching, though perhaps it's interesting that of all the horrors of George Denbrough's shocking chapter one 'death-by-dismemberment' and Patrick Hocksetter's flying leeches, the ones that haunt me most happen just off camera—the children who fall into the water-tank and are left in the dark to swim until they can't anymore, or the toddler whose father murders him with a hammer, as we learn from a police statement.

There is a lot of death, and true to life, often the threat comes from those closest to us, those who should care for us most. One of the central rules of 'safe' horror is that neither the kid nor the pet will get murdered. King not only gleefully shreds that page of the rule book, he does so while insisting, sometimes, at least, that it's precisely those charged to protect you who will do the greatest harm.

The book also presents a history of prejudice, up to the then-current day of 1985. Shocking, vile racism, from the hatred of Henry Bowers for Mike Hanlon (a mirror of his father's fury at his black neighbour), Eddie's mother's casual, 'acceptable' race 'realism,' back to the fire at The Black Spot, where King puts the boot into the notion that Klan-style violence was an exclusively Southern concern. Then there is the homophobic murder of a gay man. Throughout the narrative, King shows us the monsters of the mind that haunt so much of the American experience.

Art imitates life.

Here's the thing though—*IT* is not a fucking metaphor. It isn't. Henry Bowers was always going to end a fucked up kid and a bully because his dad was a crazy, racist asshole, but the reason he attempts to carve his name into Ben's stomach is not because of that—it's because he lives in a town inhabited by a creature so malevolent that it poisons the very air, groundwater, and atmosphere. Derry has all the ugliness of a large town that will never be a city, but the reason so many grotesquely horrible things keep happening there is that this creature, which feeds on fear and pain, has its psychic hooks in every single person unlucky enough to live there. *IT* is *not* a metaphor for the fears of childhood, or the alienation of kids from adults—that is present and correct and explored in this novel, but there's also a *real* creature that can read your mind and then shapeshift into whatever you fear most, which will use that moment of terrified paralysis to *eat the flesh from your young bones*. Because child-flesh is the tastiest, and scared child-flesh the scrummiest of all.

Can you comprehend how much this blew the mind of an eleven-year-old boy with an overactive imagination? This book gave me the keys to the kingdom (pun unintended) of human nature. All life was here—all the horrible things people could do to each other, and why they did them. The magic of childhood—man, I understood the magic of childhood while I was still living it, because some adult could remember it well enough that he could beam it into my brain from his house in Maine and show it to me from the outside and within. This book communicated that magic through the eyes of these amazing kids and the amazing adults they would become, and I understood getting older, and what it would mean. I saw it all, and it lifted me up and broke my heart, all at once.

And oh yes, those kids. Those wonderful, wonderful kids. The Loser's Club. My friends. Ben, Bev, Mike, Stan, Richie (lord, Richie), Eddie and Bill. My first black friend, my first Jewish friend. These kids. I remember so vividly how much I wished I could hang out with them in the Barrens in the summer of '58, drinking Coke from glass bottles, smoking Bev's pilfered cigarettes, listening to the radio playing rock 'n roll. Ah fuck it, why pretend? I *did*. My imagination was strong enough, and the writing good enough. *I was there*.

I think a part of me never fully left.

I read *IT* every winter up to the age of nineteen or twenty, and I've read it a few times since, and it's still untouchable, to me. Some of you had *Huckleberry Finn*, or *Just William*, or shit, I dunno, whoever. I had the Loser's Club. They were my people, and we stood together against the scariest fucking thing you could imagine, and though the cost was unbearably high, we prevailed, and Derry was destroyed. And we forgot because we must, except the words on the page are there, and we can go back any time we want and see each other again, young and fearless and terrified and laughing.

I haven't touched on a tenth of what makes this behemoth of a novel such a towering work of imagination. But then, I don't need to, do I? If you've got this far, you either already know, or never will.

Either way, I'm headed back to Derry again, before the year is out—back to this novel that remains as evergreen and full of life and possibility as the summer of '58 that its pages vividly invoke. I want to hear Richie doing his Kennedy impression. I want to hear Beverly laugh. I want to watch Ben watching her laugh, feeling the blush and simple, powerful love in his chest as my own. I want to build a dam with Mike and Stan and poor sweet Eddie. And I want to see that look in Bill's eyes, hear that scarily adult gravel in his voice when he says, 'It killed my fucking brother. I want to kill It.'

Go get *IT*, Big Bill. I'm right behind you.

PS—I mentioned the magic of childhood, above. The specific thing King was talking about there was the resilience of kids' minds—how they can calmly absorb and normalise horror that would send most adults gibbering to the nearest padded room for a nice medicated lie-down. It could just be a lame assertion to fuel the plot, because otherwise how do The Loser's Club not all end up in Juniper Hill? Except it's not, it's a fact, and I know, because *I read IT when I was eleven.* My guess is Dad knew it too. Thanks again, Dad.

Addendum—in the five years since this essay was published, I have read IT *twice more, enjoyed the* Part 1 *movie several times, and started a new podcast series called* Kit and IT, *where I interview various creative types about the book and the movie(s), and their influence. In other words, the obsession continues.*

THE FILM THAT MADE ME

RoboCop

To describe *RoboCop* as the greatest movie ever made is to make an observation so obvious as to be trite. This is after all the movie that set an all-time record when it received twenty-three Oscars at the 59th annual Academy Awards, losing out only in the 'Best Documentary' category (which is probably the only reason anyone is still talking about *Women - For America, For the World*). It's worth noting in passing that had the film been released in the era of DVD, no doubt a 'making of' short would have provided a clean sweep. Of course, the Academy did compensate for this by providing the special 'RoboCop award for outstanding awesomeness in every conceivable way' featuring, as we all know, the only time in Oscar history that the statuette was chrome rather than gold, and for that matter the only time it wore a helmet and carried a semi automatic pistol.

It's worth remembering that there was some minor controversy around this ceremony—some felt that it bent the rules a little to have 'Best Animated Short' won by a clip reel of all the ED-209 stop motion work cut together; and who could forget the outrage when the Italian dub of the film won 'Best Foreign Language Film', even though the Spanish version was widely considered the superior article? Nonetheless, '87 will forever be remembered, fairly, as the *RoboCop* Oscars.

The other cultural implications of this seismic film event are intimately familiar too, so I shall only mention in passing the congressional medal of honour bestowed upon Paul Verhoven, the presidential decree that no sequels, remakes, reboots, spin-offs or ancillary material of any description be allowed to be created, lest they dilute the greatness of what had been achieved (the moment when Reagan truly fulfilled his promise of being a unity president, and the achievement he is quite rightly most fondly remembered for), Roger Ebert's emotional retirement following his simple, two sentence review of the film ('There are no more worlds to be conquered. Three thumbs up.'), and, of course, the moment in 1988 when, standing on the ruins of the Berlin wall, the ex-East German commissar uttered the fateful words, 'Can we watch *RoboCop* now, please?'

What can your humble correspondent usefully say in the face of the weight of this history? Why, nothing. The most base and lazy student of the past thirty years will already be apprised of the film's might and splendour.

To have anything useful to say, we must first… forget. We must imagine. Imagine a world where this film did not receive the recognition it deserved. Where it was, perhaps, dismissed as merely another late 80s action movie, albeit with some biting social satire and good performances. One where, perhaps, Oliver Stone or Woody Allan dominated Oscar proceedings. Further, we must then imagine how that world, that alternate 1987, might look through the eyes of a child…

***

I was eleven years old when I first saw *RoboCop*.

It was the summer of 1989; the school summer holidays, to be as precise as I can manage at such distance, and I was staying at the house of my best friend, Ed, for the weekend. Ed's mother was away for most of Saturday. This was fortunate because Saturday was the day the Video Van Man came around.

To understand the Video Van Man, you have to understand rural Devon, circa 1989. Not so much a wretched hive of scum and villainy (me and my mates did our best, but there were only three of us, and only so many milk bottles to steal), as a cultural wasteland. The nearest town to the village I grew up in that had a cinema was eight miles away. When you're eleven, that might as well be the moon. The nearest video rental place was a similar, functionally impossible distance.

That's where the Video Van Man came in.

I don't know for sure if he was affiliated with an existing video rental establishment, or just a chancer with a respectably large VHS collection and a van. It didn't matter. What did matter was that, once a week, he came to the village, stopping at each house with a VCR. Don't ask me how he knew, but the bugger did—we didn't get a player until I was thirteen, and were not bothered once in all that time. Then, within two weeks of ours being hooked up, there he was. He opened the back of the van so we could all have a good peruse.

This in and of itself was a Big Deal. What elevated him from merely Big Deal to Life Changer was this—*he didn't give a fuck about age certificates.* Not a single, solitary fuck. If you were old enough to read the name of the film you wanted to rent, and prepared to relinquish the two-pound coins he wanted as payment, the VHS was yours for the week, no questions asked.

Madness.

(I discovered later that the situation was even more nefarious. Once we had a VCR at home and he noted my predilection for horror films, he granted me access to the 'hidden' drawer of 'banned' films, like *Zombie Flesh Eaters* and that one where the devil came out of a woman's ear. Had I been exposed to them at eleven rather than thirteen, I might be writing a rather different blog entry on a vastly different site, waxing lyrical about the evils of horror filmmakers and the warping effect of such infamy on young minds.

Well, probably not. I'd read *IT* by then. Still.)

Ed and I were familiar with his services, having tested the waters on a prior occasion with the delightful *Big Trouble In Little China*, which had rightly absorbed us for a weekend. But *Big Trouble...* was only a fifteen certificate, and this weekend we were determined to go All The Way. It was time to test our courage and resolve against the big red warning that read: 'Eighteen—Adults only'. What taboo could be more thrilling to cross? What depraved delights would we find inside? What deeply unsuitable sights and sounds might we encounter? Bloodshed? Butchery?

Boobs?

We scanned the library of titles with eagerness and care, but there would be, could be, only one serious contender. We'd seen the poster before, that amazing image of the cyborg stepping out of the police car, looking like the meanest thing to have ever walked creation, and that awe-inspiring minimalist tagline:

PART MAN.
PART MACHINE.
ALL COP.

We paid the man in slightly sweaty goldies, and took our prized possession back into Ed's house for immediate consumption. It was 10am, and his mother would not return to the house until at least 5pm.

It was *RoboCop* time.

Here's the problem with the next bit—I can't do it. I've seen *RoboCop* in excess of seventy times now. This is way more than twice the number of times I've seen my next most watched film (either *Pulp Fiction* or *The Sting*). I regret not a single viewing, and hope to double it or more before I die, but there is one unavoidable consequence: I can no longer accurately recreate that first viewing experience.

I was eleven, so I will have liked the gun. I will have fallen in love with the sound of his footsteps, the robotic whine and deep bass crunch of each boot hitting the floor. I must have been horrified by much of the bloodshed, especially Murphy's execution and the demise of poor old Kenny (though I also know that by the end of the weekend I would watch that same scene and cackle like a loon). The constant foul language will have delighted me, as will the commercials—I was too young to fully appreciate the satire, but I was bright and film savvy enough to realise they were supposed to be funny.

ED-209 will have delighted and repelled me in equal measure. Bob's fraternisation with a couple of 'models' will have left me thoroughly flustered and amazed. His death will have confirmed that the greatest two villains to grace a movie screen were Clarence Boddicker and Dick Jones. Beyond that, all I can tell you is this: as soon as the credits rolled, we'd stopped the tape and hit rewind.

We needed to see it again.

We watched *RoboCop* fourteen times that weekend (yeah, we were eleven, we counted). We watched until the second Ed's mum walked in, and from the minute she went to bed until we couldn't keep our eyes open (around 2am). She went out after breakfast on Sunday morning, and we hit play again.

We watched it. We rewound it. We slow mo'd. We frame advanced. We replayed lines of dialogue over and over, trying to replicate the cadence and timbre perfectly (to this day, I have a pretty decent, 'Dead or alive, you're coming with me,' and my, 'Well I guess we're going to be friends after all… Richard,' was perfect until my voice dropped), and sometimes just for laughs. After all, when you're eleven, watching a man repeatedly yell the words 'Fuck me!' with increasing aggression and disbelief as he plugs round after round into the bullet proof metal chest of the hardest android to grace the silver screen (sorry *Bladerunner*, sorry *Terminator*, but 1987 just called to say *RoboCop* can kick both your asses), before he is punched through the glass door of a refrigerator as he fails to flee the scene? That is *never* not funny.

And I lived the proof of it.

Frame advance is also how I know that the effect on the ED-209 gun was achieved by interspersing frames of the 'flame' firing (complete with tiny flames shooting from side exhausts to the main barrel) with beams of solid white to create a strobe effect. It is *also* the reason I can report with moral certainty that in that same scene, as Kenny is repeatedly shot with high calibre rounds and his chest and stomach explode with blood, his tie is actually blown into the air by one squib *only to be blown in half by a second squib within twelve or fourteen frames.*

I need those of you with a passing familiarity of movie effects (especially pre-digital effects) to just sit there a moment and contemplate in silent awe the enormity of what I've just described. Think about the care, the love, and the sheer perverted joy that must have gone into even attempting that effect, let alone pulling it off.

Suffice to say, by the time my exhausted, bloodshot-eyed self had been returned to my rightful parental guardian at the end of the weekend, I was as certain as a human being can be that I had seen the greatest movie ever made.

But, you know, I was eleven. What did I really know?

As it turns out—everything.

Because here's the thing about *RoboCop*, kids. Here's the great truth I have learned and relearned over and over again, since that fateful weekend in the summer of '89. This film ain't *Braveheart*, and it ain't *The Goonies*, and it sure as shit ain't T*he Lost Boys*. What I'm saying here is that *RoboCop* is The Real Deal. It stands up. Over and over.

It is, in fact, the greatest movie ever made... and here's the proof.

First—it's the greatest action movie ever made. Full stop. Oh really? You're not sure about that? Well, by all means, let's look at the competition...

- *Lethal Weapo*n? Please. Riggs fails to take the shot on Joshua. He has a good three to four seconds—plenty long enough to start cracking wise—before he's snuck up on and disarmed—and he blows it. Compare this to *RoboCop* dealing with Mr. Would-be-rapist. Case closed.

- *Face/Off*? Warmer, but here's the problem; ultimately, in *Face/Off* the characters are just chess pieces, moved about the plot on pre-determined courses to facilitate one admittedly gorgeous action scene after another. If you doubt me, consider the entirely superfluous 'oh, I just realised we haven't had a speedboat chase yet' finale, or the nauseating 'hey I lost my son, but I will instead adopt the son of my actual son's killer (and also the man who has effectively raped my wife for the last few weeks) and my wife will be cool with that because *that's how people work*.' I mean, lovely action sequences, but blerg.

- *Terminator/Terminator 2*? Here's the problem with those choices—Arnie is only good as a wooden robotic character because he is, in real life, a wooden robotic character. In T2, when 'real stuff' happens, he's woefully inadequate for the task, and *The Terminator* lacks anything like that amazing moment when Peter Weller says, 'I can feel them... but I can't remember them.'

- *First Blood/Rambo*?
    o *First Blood* is a fine, fine film. But ultimately, the 'action' part is the least important, and not what defines the film as important or good. That is entirely down to the closing fifteen minutes of the movie, when John Rambo finally collapses into a gibbering heap, recounting fractured stories of fallen comrades and his return home, as the PTSD that's driven the sorry narrative finally unravels him, and the broken-down vet from Springsteen's *Born In The U.S.A.* is made flesh before our disbelieving eyes. A great movie?

Absolutely. The best action movie? Nah. Not the point.
- *Rambo*, the fourth movie in the franchise, suffers from the opposite problem. If we were to discuss 'purest action movie,' a strong case could be made. But pure does not equate to best.

- *Die Hard*. Okay, you know what? This is a serious contender, and worthy of respect. *Die Hard* features wall-to-wall outstanding performances, brilliantly choreographed action set pieces flowing effortlessly and logically, sublime pacing, and supremely satisfying plotting. Plus Alan Rickman and Bruce Willis at the height of their powers. You know what it doesn't have? 'You have twenty seconds to comply.'

Your argument is invalid.

'Okay, Kit, you got us, *RoboCop* is the best action movie. Fine, conceded. But best movie full stop?'

Fair point. But here's the thing about *RoboCop*. It isn't *just* the best action movie ever made. It's also the best satire ever made. As the following comparisons will amply demonstrate...

- *Dr. Strangelove*? Okay, show me the bit in *Dr. Strangelove* where there's a massive shootout in a cocaine factory. I can wait... *forever*, because it's not there!

- *Burn After Reading*? I'll grant it's got the funniest punchline, but you have to slog through the 120 minutes of shaggy-dog setup to get there. Also, no, 'Nuke 'em!'

- *The Big Lebowski*? It's funnier, I'll freely allow, but not actually a satire. Also, at no point does anyone say, 'I'd buy that for a dollar!'

But I'm not done. In addition to being the best action movie *and* the best satire, *RoboCop* is *also*, and at the same time, the best *satire of an action movie.*

What's that you say? *Last Action Hero*?

As the kids used to say, 'LOL.'

'Okay Kit, you got it. The best action movie, the best satire, and the best satire of an action movie. Sounds like this *RoboCop* movie might actually be a bit of a thing, but…'

But nothing, I'm not done. There's one final category in which *RoboCop* is objectively the best film ever made, and it's the clincher. Ready?

RoboCop is… the best horror movie ever made.

I can hear your incredulous gasp from here, and you haven't even read this yet because I'm still typing (why, yes, now you come to mention it, I do have some game). I think I may even detect some indignant spluttering. Perchance, the odd harrumph. But please, consider the evidence…

- *Don't Look Now*? All chat, no trousers. 'Ooh, a little person in a red coat!' Big deal.

- *The Texas Chainsaw Massacre*? This movie has a killer rep, but it's a smokescreen. Bodycount talks, BS walks. So long, Leatherface.

- *The Exorcist*. Again, it's a good horror movie. But where is the moment in *The Exorcist* when a man drives into a vat of toxic waste, tumbles from the rear of his van, shuffles up to a colleague with his skin *melting off his body* while gibbering 'helllllp me?' (only without the 'p' sound because his lips have swollen/melted so badly he can't even talk properly), to be rejected by said colleague and ultimately killed by a speeding car going so fast that the weakened state of the body causes, on impact, his head to roll over the roof of the car as his legs collapse underneath and blood washes over the windscreen? Fucking *nowhere*, that's where. For that shit, you need *RoboCop*. In *RoboCop*, you have that.

- You also have:
    - Metal fist spikes driven through necks
    - Visceral body shock horror—Murphy's execution scene is as brutal and sadistic as anything in *Hostel*, and with a thousand per cent more point
    - A man shot through the knees and then executed by *timed grenade*
    - ED-209 shooting an innocent man for over thirty seconds (assuming you have

THE FILM THAT MADE ME

> the director's cut) while his corporate colleagues watch, helpless
> o Oh yeah, also, it's basically a retelling of the original horror story—*Frankenstein*. So there's that.

There's also that aforementioned death by toxic waste. Sidebar: That actor would go on to play by far the most interesting character in the entire 734 season run of ER *(Ed: Is this right? It felt that long…)*. This character would lose a hand to a freak accident with a helicopter, and later die by having that same helicopter *dropped on his head*. Thanks to *RoboCop*, that remains only the second strangest death this actor has depicted).

Blam! Best horror movie ever. Fact.

'Blimey Kit, that's pretty comprehensive. Anything else?'

Nnnnnnnn… yes. Actually, yes. *RoboCop* is also the finest comedy horror movie ever made. Because *Young Frankenstein* isn't actually scary, *Scream* isn't actually funny, and *Scary Movie* is neither scary nor funny.

And here's the thing. Being the best action movie, satire, satire of an action movie, horror movie, and comedy horror movie doesn't merely mean the film is five times better than its nearest rival. Oh no. Because those rivals were only trying to be one thing: *RoboCop* tries, and succeeds, at being the best at five different categories of movie *at the same time.* That's not five times more difficult, that's *exponentially* five times more difficult.

I can see I'm losing some of you. Not to worry,

MY LIFE IN HORROR VOLUME I

I've created this handy pie chart comparison which I think illustrates my point with greater clarity:

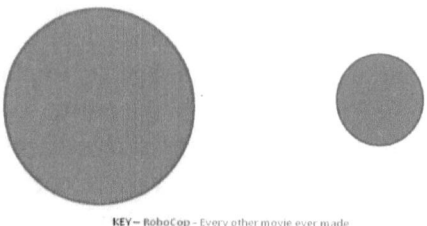

Things that make RoboCop awesome vs. things that make ever other movie ever made awesome

KEY— RoboCop - Every other movie ever made

There you have it. I haven't even scratched the surface of the universe of awesome represented in the above chart. The essential goofiness of Murphy, that makes his humanity apparent and also provides the bridge to his horrifically altered state, when the gun trick he learned to impress his son becomes the way his ex-partner realises who RoboCop really is. The hard-bitten black desk sergeant rising above cliché thanks to character-actor Robert DoQui's transcendent performance. The sound! The sound of those metallic boots hitting the ground, the background whine of robotics, the awesome boom of the military grade firepower OCP gives to the gangsters set loose to destroy RoboCop. The harsh robotic intonation of ED-209 informing the hapless Kenny (they killed Kenny!) that he has five seconds to comply, never mind that he complied seventeen seconds ago and in another four will be shot to hamburger. The fact that the robot shoots until running out of ammo because 'the future of urban

THE FILM THAT MADE ME

pacification' is a flaky piece of shit that doesn't work properly due to the creator being too busy kissing Pentagon ass and promising spare parts for the next twenty years to care about whether or not it worked.

I could go on and on and on and on and on. For as long as you're buying, I'll tell you how awesome *RoboCop* is, and when your wallet is empty, and the bar dry, and my liver failing, I'll still have more to say.

Because it's the best fucking movie made. Fact.

It's also the movie that made me.

THE ALBUM THAT MADE ME

Appetite for Destruction

It's June, 1989. I am eleven years old.

It's towards the ass end of the school term, probably the last week of school before the break, it's a glorious summer day in Devon, and no one gives a shit anymore—least of all the teachers. The borderline-sociopath headteacher who also runs the classroom for the ten and eleven year olds with an iron fist has spent most of the last few days holed in the staff room watching the cricket—if Louise Thompson is to be believed, he stands, cricket bat in hand, as if he's invented the Wii sports cricket sim seventeen years early, or, more likely, drunk. When I leave the school in a couple of weeks, I'll unaccountably shake his hand, tears not quite held back, in as pure a display of Stockholm Syndrome as you'll see, but now I'm supremely comfortable and secure in my undying hatred and contempt for him and all he stands for.

Anyway. It's summer and school's almost out, so 'class' is outdoors. 'Class' in this case equates to 'fucking about as much as you want' within wide parameters. Ed and Bev (not their real names) are here. Ed has brought, by prior arrangement, a battered twin speaker cassette radio. Bev has The Prize—a cassette tape borrowed from her impossibly cool sixteen-year-old sister. They assure me I will love it.

They have no fucking idea.

Ed hits play, and within seconds there's drums and guitars like I've never known, singing and swearing I'd have thought would be heavily restricted if not outright banned, and a primal energy that bypasses intellect and speaks—no, howls—directly to my gut.

GnR Lies changed everything.

The crowd roared like a pack of wild bears (yeah, wild bears, fuck you, I was eleven). I pictured a dust-filled stadium in the middle of the desert, a merciless sun beating on a surging sea of drunken hairy flesh, rippling, tidal, alive.

Hey fuckers! Fucken guns and fucken roses!

The drums attack like gunshots and then *everything*, two guitars and bass cranked to infinity, hit the same pattern, blistering pace, raw fucking attitude firing from the speakers. And that's before the first vocal kicks in. As soon as it does... man, I'm living a new life. I've crossed over.

Nothing will ever be the same.

So *Lies* started it. Through Bev's older sister, next came Skid Row, then W.A.S.P. (about whom more soon). And, you know, I was eleven, still with one foot in the pop world. There was a memorable period where one of my three C-90 cassettes had Skid Row's debut on one side and New Kids On The Block *Hanging Tough* copied on the other. I have no intention of defending that, though I can't help but marvel in passing at the suppleness of the mind that could listen to the closing strains of 'Hold On', fast forward, flip, and then nod along with equal pleasure to 'Big Guns'.

Something had shifted, though, for sure. Something seismic. In months, pop had been uprooted—if the guitars weren't cranked to antisocial levels, if the hair wasn't long, if there were no leather jackets or swearing or attitude, then brother, you were no longer playing my song. NKOTB got recorded over (I think with Bon Jovi's *New Jersey* opus, though that may be wrong), much to the fury of my sister, and I renounced my former taste with all the proto-fascist zeal of the true believer convert.

It was 1989. It started with *Lies*. Of course it was going to end up with *Appetite.*

It took a while, though. For starters, Noel Streak let me down. At the start of term we'd made friends in the top set maths class we'd somehow fluke-tested into, and he'd promised that if I gave him a blank tape he'd get it recorded. This was early in the September term of '89. By February '90, with me asking him every single week in every single maths class, I got the distinct impression I wasn't going to get my tape back soon.

Luckily, Ed had it on vinyl. One loan and serious nagging of mum later, and it had been transferred to c-90. Of course, I don't need to tell you that the running time was such that the album didn't quite fit on the forty-five minutes of tape, and the last song had to be put on the other side. Luckily, *Lies* eight tracks ran short.

THE ALBUM THAT MADE ME

Synchronicity.

I wasn't allowed to listen to the album that night. It was too late. So, as any self respecting child would, I took the tape to my room, stayed awake until mum went to bed, then got out my headphones and jacked in. And holy fucking shit. From the opening of 'My Michelle', that gentle picking guitar pattern that held so much menace, the second guitar's delicate melody line, that ominous bass step off, the sinister cymbal washes, I knew...

Wait, what? Oh, right. Yes, that deserves an explanation.

So some of you with a passing familiarity with the text might fairly be pointing out that the opening song on *Appetite For Destruction* is not 'My Michelle', but 'Welcome To The Jungle'. And you would be correct, at least in the narrow, literal sense. But it's 1990. We're not digital, we're analogue, and my mum, God love her, is as analogue as it gets. She's so analogue, in fact, that when a band (in a fit of branding genius arguably slightly ahead of its time) decides to label its vinyl release not 'Side A' and 'Side B' or 'Side 1' and 'Side 2' but 'Side G' and 'Side R'... Well, it's dogs and cats lying together. Confusion reigns. And I end up with a C-90 where the album is recorded the wrong way around.

Only, turns out I didn't. Turns out, in point of fact, that I ended up as being one of the few fortunate people who actually had *Appetite For Destruction* the right way round.

Think about it. We open with 'My Michelle'. The guitars and cymbals swirl with sinister intent, slowly building, and when the pattern ends, there's a snare hit the likes of which you haven't heard since 'Like A Rolling Stone' (or if you're eleven, fucking ever) and bam! The song erupts, an out-of-control freight train of a riff, sparks flying, rage ringing out of every tortured string, and the literally-screaming vocal, impossibly, inhumanly high, kicks in:

> *Your Daddy works in porno*
> *now that mommy's not around*
> *she used to love her heroin*
> *but now she's underground…*

I mean, holy fucking mother of God could there be a more brutal, direct statement of intent, a stronger slap in the face? This is *Appetite For Destruction*, motherfucker—get on board or get the fuck out of the way.

So I'm lying in the dark of my single bed, eleven, eyes clenched shut, wanting to block everything except the enormous sound engulfing my brain. And next it's 'Think About You', and I never knew a love song could be so fast, so loud, and the closing minor key flurry leaves me breathless, as love becomes a desperate longing need. And then it's the intro to 'Sweet Child O' Mine' and I'm convinced I've heard the greatest guitar playing I'll *ever* hear—a conviction that holds true and unshaken for all of four minutes, before the final guitar solo of the same song, when Slash effortlessly takes his place in the all-time rock guitarist hall of fame with a solo so sublime, so perfect, I will hear it long after I go deaf.

We're only three songs in.

THE ALBUM THAT MADE ME

Next is 'You're Crazy', which I know from *Lies*, but here it's twice the pace and eleven million times the volume and I'm lying flat on my back headbanging, even though it doesn't really work, because I can't fucking not. And then it's 'Anything Goes', a song that for years I assume is about losing your virginity (because of the opening line 'I've been thinkin' 'bout, thinkin' 'bout sex/ Always hungry for somethin' that I haven't had yet'—and yeah, go ahead and laugh, but again, I was eleven) with the sleaziest guitar I'd ever heard.

Then 'Rocket Queen'—more menace, more razor wire vocals and lyrics, the closing coda singing love but sounding hateful, brutal. And then, and then…

…after all that, after the stall has been well and truly set and the manifesto read, then and only then, they drop The Big One.

You are finally ready for 'Welcome To The Jungle'.

I'm not one of those people who say point blank that 'Welcome To The Jungle' is the greatest rock 'n roll song ever written. What I will say, with the seriousness of a heart attack, is that any discussion of a *potential* 'greatest rock 'n roll song' that doesn't give serious consideration to 'Welcome To The Jungle' is not a conversation worthy of your all-too-brief time.

It's fucking amazing. The intro is like Michael Jackson's 'Thriller' grew some hair on its balls, and when the snare booms and the main riff kick in, if your head ain't nodding, you're already dead. Everything you've heard over the last side of music is distilled to its rawest essence on one track. It's the desperate, hungry, gaping need, the brutality, the rage and frustration of someone *just* smart enough to see the size and shape of the bullshit hole they're trapped in without being *quite* smart enough to see a way out, the displacement of that rage onto another ('You can taste the bright lights/ But you won't get them for free'), that helpless fury lashing out with venom and razor sharp observation, cutting deep and sparing no one. And that's before Slash unleashes another laid back masterpiece of a solo, not a note misplaced, every bend and flurry perfectly timed and chosen, and the breakdown before the final chorus pounds the toms and Axl screams with the conviction of the damned:

> *You know where you are?*
> *You're in the jungle, baby!*
> *You're gonna diiiiiie!*

And then we're off to Fuck You City with 'It's So Easy', crunching, crushing dead eyed nihilism, as Axl's vocal drops into near-human range for the first time and the raw ugliness of the LA scene is ripped from California and beamed directly into the mind of an eleven-year-old boy in North Devon. Everything is fucked, everything and everyone is ugly, and the narrator's own paranoia feels dangerous, infectious.

From there, we're given the flip side of the same scene, this time in anthem form. 'Nighttrain' is a rollicking celebration of getting shitfaced and rolling out (ah, but doesn't the darkness come back, towards the end, as another mind-blowing guitar solo takes the riff to the minor key, and the refrain turns ragged, desperate—'I guess I guess I guess I never learn')?

'They're Out To Get Me', ostensibly written about the LAPD but actually about my year seven Geography teacher, takes us to 'Mr. Brownstone', another riff you have a hard time believing was written by mortals, rather than just hewn from the cliff face of the raw universe.

And then... then you have to turn the tape over for the grand finale—'Paradise City'.

For the next two years, I would listen to that recording of *Appetite For Destruction* at least once a day. The contours of the songs are etched into my brain, and I can drop the needle and hear the whole thing, with perfect clarity, any time I want. In a real and direct sense it is a part of me. Example? I wrote this whole thing without listening to the album once. Well... without playing it, anyway.

Appetite For Destruction is an ugly, loud, rage fuelled, misogynistic, drug induced, and yes, flawed album. No surprise—It was made by arrogant and deeply flawed men, in a time and place when casual misogyny and rape culture were even more deeply ingrained than they are now. It's not that this album couldn't be made today—it's more than it probably wouldn't be. And genuinely, I take that as a sign of progress, and I'm grateful for it.

But there's something else too, something this album has that not just redeems it but makes it transcendent. See, the ugly truth that *Appetite* exposes is this: flawed, broken people sometimes make great art. And this is one of those times. Because all the ugliness and bitterness and spite and hate and bile and, yeah, horror, are heartfelt and honestly expressed. Axl Rose is clearly a deeply unpleasant human being, but you don't need a trial to prove it—he convicts himself in every line of this record. And that has value. It exposes ugly truths that go beyond the individual. It exposes a cultural rot that is real and deep and puss-filled and toxic and gross. The fact that the author is apparently at best indifferent to, and at worst actively embraces that rot matters not a jot. In exactly the way that Conan Doyle's faithful representations of the views of the time expose, like a raw nerve, the vile and reprehensible hypocrisy of the Victorian age and attendant class structure and values, the lyrics of Axl Rose stand as a monument to the nihilistic, misanthropic ugliness of the Hollywood rock scene of the mid to late 80s. You feel it on a visceral level, and the album allows you, for forty-seven minutes, to see the world though that myopic lens. It's disturbing and exhilarating, and in part disturbing *because* it's so exhilarating—so raw, so vital—like a really good horror movie or novel, say. That he also has a voice, which is (or was) one of the greatest instruments in rock music, and no small skill at songwriting, is not in opposition to that fact. The one facilitates the other. And you wouldn't need to know a single thing about *Use Your Illusion* or *Chinese Democracy* to know how this story ends—the inevitable tragedy/farce that Guns N' Roses will become is written into the very DNA of the band.

They were always going to burn out, rise too high, too fast. All of their wishes would be granted, and the same flaws that drove them to make this record would tear them to pieces—just add money and fame, results guaranteed. There's an inevitability to it that borders on natural justice. They got, in the end, exactly what they deserved. *Appetite For Destruction*—the clue's in the name.

But oh my loves, how bright the flame did burn in 1990. Bright enough to shine clear across a continent and an ocean, sending sparks into the belly of an eleven-year-old boy in a tiny village in North Devon, ensuring his world would forever be bigger, louder, and angrier. It burns here still.

Lies was the beginning. But *Appetite For Destruction* will always be the album that made me.

PRIMARY YEARS

0 – 11

MINDS IMMEASURABLY SUPERIOR TO OURS

Jeff Wayne's War of the Worlds

One thing I noticed as I came to pull these columns together for publication is that the content is pretty evenly split between personal expressions of joy and horror. This makes sense—I love horror, but at the same time, duh, it's horrific. And the sheer breadth with which I cast my net when using that term has become part of the game, as you'll discover.

So there's a lot of darkness in what follows, but I'm really glad that we start with joy; an unexpected contemporary experience that opened a deep well of childhood memory, from an album first released in the year of my birth.

It's the 20th February 2016, and for my sins I am thirty-seven years of age. I'm at the Dominion theatre in the West End of London, due to a happy accident involving my father scoring some overseas work at short notice and a non-refundable ticket. In attendance is my stepmother.

The stage dressing is beautiful. A safety curtain with the name of the show projected onto it prevents any view of the performance area, but the clockwork scrolling up and across the arch, gold effect on red, is gorgeous. And the logo, as we both remark, is iconic.

That said, overall my expectations are low. For one thing, I have a huge attachment to much of the original cast, and most of them are not in attendance (and not all of the ones that are will be playing the roles they did previously). For another, well, I basically don't like musicals. At all. Rock operas, fine, but sing all the time or don't sing at all is my basic philosophy, mainly because in practice the typical broadness of the non-singing performances sets my teeth on edge, and I find the transition from one to the other not just goofy but grating. And no, this isn't a musical, more like a narrated pop opera, so we'll probably be fine, but on the other hand, it's the West End, so they're probably contractually obliged to have interpretive dance at some point, so blah.

And then, the lights go down…

…and the screen goes up.

And Liam Neeson starts talking.

And all of a sudden it's… 1983 or '84, and I am somewhere between four and six years old, perched in front of the speakers of a record player. A man starts talking to me in a rich baritone about the Timeless Whorls Of Space and Creatures That Swarm And Multiply In A Drop Of Water, and the gorgeous language, gorgeously spoken, washes over me as I stare at the picture of the tripod on the cover, shooting out some kind of laser that's melting a boat. As my mind boggles at the image and reels from the half understood implications of what the voice is telling me…

DUN DUN DUNNNNNN!

2016: Holy shit! There's every chance that it's been twenty years since I last heard those notes, played on those instruments. It's a hammer blow to the soul. No, an internal explosion—a burst of light in my gut and brain. I feel like I'm giving off sparks, and my mouth pulls into a grin, big and goofy.

Then the drums come in, good and loud, and I glance over to the left, seeing the band lined on their own podium, opposite the strings. In the centre, the conductor does his thing, keeping them all honest. The mix is not perfect: it's a bit bass heavy, and for what I can well imagine will be the only time in my adult life, I find myself wishing the synth was louder. The counterpoints to the strings get a bit lost in the mix, not as front and centre as they were in the recording—a recording that is now unspooling in my mind in sync with the live performance. And as the overture ends, and the timelessly weird pitch-shifting radar sound kicks in, I'm flung back in time once more.

1987—We have the cassette. The double cassette. I listen to it endlessly, on the big stack system in our living room. I cut out the coupon in the inlay card, and persuade my mother to send it off with a postal order for £2 to get the 'full colour booklet, featuring additional artwork!' It takes long enough to arrive that I forget completely about it. Then an A4 envelope arrives. I open it, mystified, and cry with delight when that huge picture of the tripod melting the boat comes into view, with that amazing logo.

I look through it over and over again, staring at the huge painted art as the story unfolds. The image of the evacuation of London stays with me—there's a woman in a Victorian dress, bleeding from a head wound, eyes staring ahead with blind terror. Further back, part of a crowd, a portly gentleman in a suit and whiskers has his arms up in a puffing run. Behind them both, behind them all, a tripod fires a heat ray at a building, causing an explosion and raining down rubble. I consider taking the pictures out and making them into posters for my wall.

2016: Wait, what? There's a new song. It's... not very good. It's about people being excited about the coming of the Martians, full of 'hope and joy and kittens' or something, and it's bad for two reasons. One, it sounds like a typical musical number from a typical musical, which means it is horrendously out of place here, and two, it's ahistorical—by which I mean, there is zero chance that Victorian England responds to the arrival of spaceships from Mars with joy and hope and expectation—we're strictly a fixed bayonets and cannon nation at this point. I mean, there's even kids going 'wee-oo-wee-oo!' to mimic that awesome weird radar, only without the pitch shifting. It's bad, and I can only suppose a running time insert to make act one last the full hour.

In fairness, part of why it grates is that I am waiting for that amazing, plunky, woody bass line that kicks off the opening of the cylinder. Luckily, it's not a long delay, and when it arrives, it's every bit as transporting as I'd hoped.

1989—I'm still listening. New house, and I have a stereo in my bedroom now, and that means headphones. The voice speaks directly into my brain. I'm listening at night, too loud, and when the lid falls off, the crash makes me jump. The build through the narration into the main body of music, wah wah plus vocoder plus sound effects and synth, is glorious—like, *Dark Side Of The Moon* glorious.

2016: It's all kicking off now. Looking nervous for three or four minutes in coordinated interpretive dance can be nobody's idea of a good time, but they do it well. Still, I can't take my eyes off the band.

At least until the heatray starts up.

I'm three rows from the front when it lights up, and a sheet of flame ignites at the front of the stage. It's big enough to make me sweat. Behind it, as the guitar plays the theme, the dancers writhe and fall, while on the screens behind the performers, the nozzle of the heatray spins and glares, and figures engulfed in flames collapse. It's full on, but even when we slip back to the dream sequence, my main attention returns to the band. Because I'm in the same room as people making this music, and I just can't quite believe it. They are amazing—note perfect, tight as anything, assured. It's a surreal experience.

The expanded version is interesting—there's additional narration, but I'm unconvinced it was needed. And it's grossly unfair, but Liam Neeson is no Richard Burton. Having him appear as a projection onto screens, while his onstage counterpart pulls all the singing duties, is an odd choice, but one that works well in practice, mostly. There's a brilliant moment—actually more brilliant in retrospect, because at the time it was so fast I hardly had time to notice it—when the narrator plunges into water, and for a moment, the sound of the music becomes washy and distorted, before breaking back in as he surfaces.

The visuals are stunning—and yes, a physical tripod makes an appearance, crab walking across the stage and shooting smoke and light. It should be utterly absurd, but it is not. In fact, it's awesome.

And then 'Forever Autumn' starts, and I am a child again, listening, eyes shut, headphones delivering the acoustic guitars and strings directly into my mind, and I feel my throat tightening, and 2016 me has time to think, 'really?' And then the singer hits this line, note perfect:

Like the sun through the trees, you came to love me,
Like a leaf on the breeze you blew away...

I am astonished by the tears I feel on my cheeks. Amazing.

And I guess it's equal parts a perfect marriage of lyrical theme and music—the poetry may not be subtle, but bloody hell it's on the nose; not an ounce of fat, elegant almost unto perfection—and that this is likely to be the first song that ever broke my heart, long before I'd be mature enough to understand what that meant.

Then we're back to the collapse, 'the rout of civilisation,' as the narrator has it. I think about the supposedly modern obsession with disaster porn stories—*The Walking Dead, 2012* and all the rest of it—and reflect that so few of them get at the sheer desperation expressed in this passage of music and narration. When the theme dissolves back into 'Forever Autumn', as the narrator sees his wife swept away on the boat, before transitioning seamlessly back to the main overture theme, we've just been given an object lesson in how the personal and global can superimpose on each other—one a microcosm of the other, the smaller tragedy hooking us into the wider catastrophe. The solo in 'Thunderchild' is glorious, wiry, wailing, desperate.

How much of that was I actually thinking as I sat there, listening to the sinking of 'Thunderchild'? None of it. How much of it was I feeling?

All of it.

The narrator's wife escapes, but the earth belongs to the Martians.

End of act one.

Bloody hell.

I get up on not entirely stable legs, and complete the genuflection of capitalism at the merch stall. Yes, the T-shirt *and* the mug. What can I say? At least I stopped short of the keyring.

Part 2 opens with a reprise of 'Forever Autumn' that I frankly could have done without, and then we're off into 'Red Weed'. I have to admit to having a certain curiosity about how they'd handle this—a lengthy section of at times profoundly odd music with little narration. And the answer is about what you'd expect—lots of CGI footage of the red weed crawling over the English countryside, with people dancing in profoundly odd costumes. It's technically flawless, and genuinely eerie, but I'm basically a philistine, and if I'm honest, would rather have just watched the band playing—especially the wonderful, all-too-brief guitar solo. Because the musicians continue to be astonishing, and I keep having to remind myself that I'm in the room with them.

Oh shit, here comes the parson. A favourite since childhood, this sequence. The way the theme of the 'Spirit of Man' verses combine with the 'No, Nathanial' pleading always got me. And, of course, the recording stars no less a vocal talent than Phil Lynott.

In 2016, we get Jimmy Nail.

And I'm not one of Those People. Jimmy Nail is a talented actor, a decent writer, and he's got his vocal range. But fucking hell, you're talking about taking on a part played by one of the greatest rock singers of the last half-century. It's just not fair, and he tries, but… it *really* doesn't work. I mean, it's not quite egregiously bad, but it's a weak moment—the acting as well as the vocal performance. And I sympathise—it's a tough part, and I'm sure part of the reason Lynott's performance of the spoken word works as well as it does is because we don't have to watch him. You can get away with a broadness of performance in radio that might be a problem even on stage. But it's like he just can't quite commit to chewing the scenery enough to land it, which is a shame.

Oh, by the way, this is the part of the story where we discover the Martians are capturing live humans to hold them in cages and drain them of their blood to feed on it. Just in case you're wondering how this is *My Life In Horror*. I mean, bloody hell, it's bleak.

Anyhow, Jimmy Nail's performance has made me nervous, because coming up, I remember we have 'Brave New World'. And that song contains a vocal performance that is, to use a technical term, impossible. I mean, David Essex managed it, back in his prime, but he's not even going to be attempting it this evening. That dubious honor goes to Daniel Bedingfield, about whom I know nothing. That is, his acting in Act One was good, but I haven't heard him sing.

And he nails it. Knocks it out of the park. It's a superb performance. You feel like he really gets it—he understands the bravado and triumphalism that sound so impressive but are ultimately brittle, and predicated on a fantasy, a pipe dream (pun, I guess, intended). For me, there's echoes of every chickenhawk speech about the glory of arms, every politician that's talked about a hand up rather than a hand out, a deep hypocrisy that could either be rooted in venal self serving rhetoric or actual delusion. Ultimately, there's no way of knowing, and ultimately, we're fucked either way. There's the unmistakable echo of the jackboot under the triumphalist march.

Just think of all the poverty, the hatred and the lies,
And then imagine the destruction of all that you despise...

If that doesn't give you the willies, I strongly suggest you read more speeches from history. Yikes.

The lyrics are utterly brilliant, carrying all this ambiguity effortlessly, and Bedingfield puts it right in the back of the net. 'I've got a plan.' Indeed.

After the show, I discovered in the program that Jeff Wayne thinks the story of *War Of The Worlds* is ultimately one of hope. As a childhood fan of this story, I find that utterly boggling. I mean, civilisation is destroyed, technological terror is rained down on the survivors, who are rounded up and harvested for their blood, and in the end we only survive because indifferent microbes, germs, wipe out our invaders. Our salvation is finally down to the fact that we've evolved an immunity to the forces on our planet that have been out to kill us from day one. If that's a message of hope, it's an odd one. Feels more like fatalism, to me. Even more strangely, is this song, 'Brave New World', which Wayne cites as being his chief justification for this perspective, quoting the following lines:

> *Take a look around you,*
> *At the world we used to know.*
> *Does it really seem much more,*
> *Than a crazy circus show?*
> *But maybe from the madness,*
> *Something beautiful may grow...*

And if that's hope, okay, but man, it's fragile, and precarious, and expressed by someone whose idea of what 'something beautiful' means is diametrically opposed to mine. Which ultimately speaks to the incredible strength of the writing—the fact that it can bear the weight of two such different interpretations.

It's been a day for surprises, but I think 'Brave New World', the performance and the lyric, is the biggest. Certainly, it's still rattling around in my head now, days later.[1]

The rest of the show plays out as expected, and to my delight, they keep the NASA ending, replete with a final attack from that ridiculous, wonderful tripod prop. And somehow, I'd missed the blindingly obvious. Because when the curtain call is complete, and the musicians have taken their bow, the conductor finally leaves his podium and turns to face us.

And it's Jeff fucking Wayne.

I leap to my feet, clapping so hard I can feel the impact right up to my shoulders, and I'm far from alone—there are people jumping up all around me. There are tears in my eyes, again. Jeff Wayne. I've just watched and heard *A Musical Version of The War Of The Worlds* conducted by the composer. A man who probably deserves equal credit with the Doctor as the reason for my continued love of and interest in SF. And, you know, the Doctor is only real in my head.

Jeff Wayne.

Thank you. Thank you.

It was… it is—you are—bloody magnificent.

PS—It's August 2015, and following the boarding of the loft, the epic emptying of the garage has begun. Boxes are opened and contents sifted, assigned to

---

[1] *In 2019, this all feels nightmarishly prescient. Oh, to go back to a pre-Brexit, pre-Trump world. Alas.*

'keep out', 'keep in loft', and 'chuck' piles. Hoarder that I am, the 'chuck' pile is small enough to be testing the superhuman patience of my wife.

And it's either a boxfile or a smaller carton we're working through, and in amongst old Guns and Roses posters and Private Eye back issues, she holds up a folded brochure and looks at me, eyebrow raised.

'Surely not this?'

I look at the tripod rising out of the sea, heatray firing at the boat. I take it from her hand and turn it over, seeing the portraits of Richard Burton, Phil Lynott, and the bios underneath.

My eyes mist over. I barely hear her sigh of resignation as she turns back to the boxes.

ALIVE, BUT LIKE A NIGHTMARE

Indiana Jones and the Temple of Doom

It's dark. Like it is at night. No... worse. We're inside, so no stars, no moon. It's the true dark of a confined space. To the sides, there's a faint green glow. Behind, if I were to look, the flickering red pinpoints, burning to yellow with the inhalation. But I probably don't look. Why would I, when what fills my field of vision is so bright?

The screen is enormous. It redefines 'big' for me in a way that life probably never tops. I mean, you spend your life looking at square CRT TV screens, and then... there's this! Gigantic, blazing bright, casting everything else into shadow. And the sound! Rumbling, roaring. You can literally, if it's desired, hear a pin drop with crystal clarity.

The inside of my mouth is a war zone—the salt of butter popcorn crashing against the sticky sweetness of the 7-up—but my mind is in perfect harmony, every sense bent to the task of absorbing the story playing out in front of me.

And it's not my first rodeo. Jedi was my first. Of that, I remember little that I can place with clarity (as opposed to the many tens of times I have seen the film since). Vader's mask glowering from the screen, dwarfing the room with its malevolent presence. Luke's green lightsaber. The crackle of lightning and fizz of the climactic duel between father and son. Little more.

But it's enough for me to understand the setting, the rules. No talking. No getting up for a wee—you'll miss something. Enough for me to have acclimatised a bit, too. The scale of the screen remains breathtaking, even awe inspiring, but it no longer causes such a severe short-circuit that the scale is all I can absorb. No, I'm ready for this one. Unlike with Jedi, this time, I'm ready.

Oh, to be six again.

Things are weird from the get-go. Why is the woman singing in a foreign language? What's with the dragon? In fact, what's with the extravagant dance routine? You can't even read the name of the movie properly; she's dancing in front of it. It's disconcerting, almost alienating. And unlike with the first movie, it does not open with our hero. Worse, when he does show, he's... well, clean. Suited and booted.

He starts talking, to a clearly bad man and his bad friends. Things deteriorate rapidly, and our hero is threatening to stab the girl in the red dress with a meat fork while the villain laughs, and then our hero's friend is shot and he's sweating and the sound goes washy and the camera goes woozy and our hero is poisoned...

And then, less than five minutes from the conclusion of the opening credits, our hero has murdered one of the henchmen by skewering him in the chest with a spit of flame-roasted meat. That is still on fire. The man screams in agony, bleeding from the chest wound, and fires a gun into the air, at which point all hell breaks loose.

I am six years old, and I am five minutes into my first horror movie.

The terror basically doesn't stop. The following action sequence is a blur of too-loud gunfire and chaotic kinetic action. I mean, the first moment I remember breathing again was the car chase, which is not the part of any movie you'd normally associate with chilling out.

But this is not like other movies.

I can still remember how much of a relief that chase was—a reassertion of what I understood an Indy movie to be, an action staple of this and Bond. Similarly, the liferaft sequence, as they leap from the plane—it helps that Indy is back in costume, of course, but mainly it just helps because it's known, familiar. Indy isn't threatening to kill a woman, no one is getting skewered or set on fire, it's just good old fashioned life-in-peril.

With the exception of the mine cart sequence, and the spike trap, it's also the last time I'll feel that way for the entire running time.

From here, it's a sheer drop into a deep pit, plunging into the dark unknown with no points of reference and handholds. This begins as soon as the life raft hits calmer waters, and Willie asks Indy how he knows they're in India.

And, okay, sidebar time: I really want to capture six-year-old me as authentically as I can, and that's going to push us into some problematic places, in no small measure because this is a problematic movie, and I was a very white kid raised in a very, very white world. My parents are both good people and not racists, so I'm fortunate not to have any of the overt hatred baggage to deal with, but at the same time, a total absence of any lived experience of people of colour whatsoever as a child meant that basically all I had was TV and movies, and at six, not a huge amount of either. I hope that my willingness to be honest and the shame I now feel at some of my reactions of the time will mitigate these reactions for you, but ultimately, that's your call to make, not mine.

Because that aged Indian man scared the crap out of me.

He was so thin. So... I'm desperately trying to avoid the word alien, because genuinely it's not quite right. I knew he was a person, I didn't think of him as 'other' in that sense, it was more... well, as I'll cover in more detail in the next essay, I had some kind of understanding of what brown skinned and thin meant, given concurrent global events, and broadly it meant Nothing Good. And I think—or maybe I just hope—that my fear came not from repulsion at The Other but more out of... a kind of empathic overload, maybe?

I vividly remember how news coverage of that Ethiopian famine fucked me up, really to this day. I can think of few things more horrifyingly bleak and hopeless than starvation, and that's inextricably linked to an early understanding that I was (and am) a child of mind boggling plenty. I mean, the guilt is functionally useless—I don't use it to make the world a better place, it just sits in a box in the well of my mind, mostly forgotten, its influence felt only in occasional spasms of petty self-sabotaging behaviour, because I know, deep down, that I deserve none of the things that make me happy—that it's all there purely because of the luck of the genetic dice roll that I was born to white parents in England and not black starving ones in Africa. And I can't remember a time I haven't known that. So, thanks again, Geldof, I guess, but also, I genuinely think that's what was going on when this skeletal brown figure with piercing eyes stared down the camera and into my soul.

Except... well, all that's true, but there is also just that I didn't know anyone that looked anything like this, and that was at best disconcerting and at worst threatening. I guess I just need to fucking own that.

Anyway.

My memory was of a series of old men like the one by the river, each pointing to the next on the horizon, until our heroes make it to the village. I can see the precise moment Indy tells Willie that this is more food than these people eat in a week. That got me, you can bet. And the way the villagers flocked around Shortround was terrifying, and sure, by the end of the sequence we know why, but the explanation happens later, and the image of all those arms, frantically reaching for the child, seeking desperately to touch, to caress...

Oh, right, Shortround. I loved him. Aw, why kid? I love him still. But back then, I really did want to be him. My childhood obsession with baseball caps ran from this movie until I turned thirteen, and Shortround is all of why. He's Indy's friend, that's the thing. An actual kid, an actual friend, not a hired hand or nephew or whatever. Is there a sweeter gig for a child adventurer in cinema history? My heart denies it. Shortround is the best.

So I remember Shortie on an elephant, and Willie flinging a snake away thinking it was the elephant, but that's kind of it for that sequence, for the simple reason that what followed is seared onto my memory.

Because fucking *hell*, that banquet.

I wasn't exactly a picky eater as a child, but I was slightly more prone than your average kid to throw up if something disagreed with me or I overate. Consequently, I had what I suppose I'd describe as some mild anxieties about eating in any kind of formal restaurant setting—an issue that still occasionally rears its head without warning, though rarely with as dire consequences as back then.

To say this movie did me no favours would be an understatement.

Snake surprise—you cut open the snake and live eels wriggle out. Which people then eat. Also scarab beetles, they eat them too, and then belch. Chilled monkey brains. Served in the skull, with a silver spoon. Are you fucking kidding me? The slurping noise the diners make when the trepanned skull cap is removed… Yup, I just made myself shudder with the memory. In this context, the eyeball soup gag is as sadistic as it is superfluous. I do not faint, but nor do I want any more popcorn or 7-up—ideally, I'd like less.

And again, I have no point of reference. As an adult, I can see the humor, but as a kid? Just terrifying, on so many levels.

And this is the fucking 'comedy' sequence—the 'hilarious' tension reliever before the real shit hits the fan.

My memory is that the spike trap didn't mess me up too badly. It was exciting, even scary, but also very Indy, somehow. We've seen death traps before, and we know how Indy rolls. Be scared, but don't be worried, I guess is what I'm saying. Same with the bugs, I suppose—we've had spiders, snakes, so, bug menagerie, okay. To be honest, with all the surrounding freakery, this thrill ride was a comfort, even as it raised my heart rate and dried my mouth. And, you know, the stab of joy as he reaches back for the hat *just in time*... I can not only remember it, I experience it every rewatch. It's a perfect moment of cinema.

From there, things go straight to hell.

I cannot do it justice. The impact was visceral. I remember the noise—the clanking chains, the drums, the chanting. And the fire, of course—the pit of lava. The sheep skull helmet. The terror on the face of the man strapped into the iron cage. The villain's hand becoming a claw as he reaches for the heart of his victim. I knew it was his heart. I could hear it beating.

Too much. Way, way too much. I closed my eyes. My memory of the last few seconds of the sequence are the clanking and rattling chains, the drums and chanting, and the audience gasps at what I later learn is the victim's beating heart bursting into flames.

Family entertainment, circa 1984.

Fuck me.

There is no overstating the degree this messed with my tiny mind. The nightmares, yes, but so much more. To this day, I have a visceral reaction to clanking chains, an involuntary physical response that traces right back to when my eyes squeezed shut in the dark of a London cinema. For all that I can wax intellectual about why *Hellraiser* is a great horror movie (and indeed, shall do later, see page **220**), I can't deny that one of the reasons the film petrifies me is because it contains that same clanking chain motif—a sound that, for me, will always be linked to existential terror.

In some ways, there's worse to come. Child slaves, voodoo, another seemingly indestructible guard in hand to hand combat with our hero... oh, and then there's the small matter of Indy turning evil.

I swear, this fucking movie.

I remember Indy being tied up, interrogated, beaten, then comes the cup made from... fuck, it's not even a skull, it's a mummified head, with the open mouth forming a spout. And of course Indy is going to get out of it somehow, going to fight off the baddies and escape... and then he doesn't. He drinks the blood, and after a nightmare sequence in a coffin shaped room full of candles, Indy turns bad and straps Willie into the fucking cage to be burned.

I realize I'm running the danger of repeating myself, but what the actual fuck?

In dramatic narrative terms, this has to be the nadir, the moment of maximum crisis—and in terms of the movie narrative, it is. This is the pivot of the entire film, the rock bottom depth—it is, literally and metaphorically, all uphill from here.

But I'm six. I don't know any of that. All I know is that the hero, *my* hero, has turned bad somehow, is about to kill the girl. Shortround runs to him, yelling, pleading, crying, and Shortround has my entire proxy, speaks for me, all my sense of outrage and fear and... not even betrayal, it's too big for that, just fucking stupefaction at this turn.

Because if you were a boy in the 80s with daddy issues—which is to say, if you were a boy in the 80s—Indy was the ultimate surrogate father figure; idealised masculinity writ large. In him, we saw our childish impulses, sure; wry humour, cynicism, greed and competitive spirit. But we also saw those traits idealised, turned into virtue by standing them in opposition to bullies, tyrants, and sadists. Indy is God-Daddy, strong, human, yet infallible, and we are his Shortround; utterly devoted, secure in our absolute faith that Indy is Good, is Right, is Just.

Shortround's outrage at this blasphemy is in entire sympathy with mine, as I stare in bug eyed horror at what unfolds.

And then Indy strikes him.

Strikes me.

We fall to the floor. The pain in our face is bad. Indy is a strong man, and while it was a slap rather than a punch, it was a powerful slap.

But that's not what hurts the most. Not even close.

What hurts, what burns, is the betrayal of trust. It's there, blazing in our eyes, refracted but not diminished by our tears. He was our hero, he was our friend. This is not him.

This can't be him.

But it was.

It was.

FEED THE WORLD

December, 1984. I am six years old.

Neither of my parents were the kind to turn off their TV's when the news came on, so I'd seen it, and I'd asked the questions kids ask. These are the ones I can remember, with the answers I recall. All, some, one, or none of them may be accurate. They feel right, though.

'Where is that?'

'Africa.'

'Why are those people brown?' I grew up in the rural north, then the rural southwest. Outside of TV and occasional trips to London to visit my Nan, I didn't see black people. At all. They were outside of my experience. I remember feeling no fear or anger or discomfort—only curiosity, and maybe a little caution.

'Because it's very hot in Africa, the sun is very hot, so their skin is brown to stop them getting sunburnt.'

It's Christmas time
There's no need to be afraid

'Why are there so many of them?'

'There's a lot of people in Africa. It's a refugee camp.'

'Why are they living in tents?'

'Because they don't have any money. There's been a drought.'

'What's a…'

'It means there's been no rain, so none of their crops have grown.'

At Christmas time
We let in light and banish shade

I know this one. Maybe from the harvest festival at school.

'So they don't have any food?'

'That's right. No water to drink, either.'

'Why are there so many children?'

'They have big families.'

'Why? If there's no food or water…'

'They didn't know. Anyway, it's traditional over there. To have big families.'

I'm remembering it wrong, guessing too much. Never mind. It feels right.

And in our world, of plenty
We can spread a smile of joy

'Why are they not moving?'

'They're too tired to move.'

'Why are they so thin?'

'Because they're starving.'

I think about that. About starving. About long car drives, being late for tea, or waking early and being late for breakfast. Hungry. Starving. No. Not starving. I look back at the TV. At the stick thin figures. Really, like a bundle of sticks under brown canvas.

I think I'll never say I'm starving again.

MY LIFE IN HORROR VOLUME I

> *Throw your arms around the world*
> *At Christmas time*

'Why do the children have such big bellies?'
'Their bellies are so empty, they've swollen up.'
'Why don't they do anything about all the flies? Brush them away?'
'They don't have enough energy. They're dying.'
Dying. Because it didn't rain and there's no food.

> *But say a prayer*
> *pray for the other ones*

I knew about praying, at six. And at six, I was probably still young enough to do it, at least at school, not having yet noticed the disconnect between what my teachers taught and what my parents lived. But the thing that got me was... food. I was surrounded by it. There were trays of it every lunch at school, bowls and plates every breakfast and dinner. Our cupboards were full of food. So were the shops.

'Why can't we send them our food? We have loads!'

Somewhere in the back of my mind, there's something about a grain mountain, from the news. Surely...

'It's complicated.'

> *At Christmas time, it's hard*
> *But, when you're having fun*

It didn't sound complicated. It sounded simple.

FEED THE WORLD

Hungry people. Spare food. Heck, it sounded *dumb*.

I think maybe my mother's answer was clearer, albeit bleaker.

'I don't know, son.'

> *There's a world outside your window*
> *And it's a world of dread and fear*

I knew that, of course. Up north, the local news had shown people fighting with police, huge crowds of each, something about mines. I'd seen men with guns, and bombs exploding, and plane crashes. There were murderers in the world, who got caught— arrested. But they'd killed first. Sometimes children. Stranger danger. There were germs. Diseases. And later... well, later there'd be Challenger and Dunblane and Columbine and 9/11.

But none of that seemed this stupid. This... pointless. This solvable. Mountain of food. Continent of starving people.

I didn't get it.

I still don't, truth be told.

> *Where the only water flowing*
> *is the bitter sting of tears*

It's not complicated. We had food. We had planes. They were children. I knew, instinctively, without being told, that this was wrong. It was... an offence. Against morality. Against the notion of humanity. I didn't have the words, but I knew this, felt it deeply. It made me cry, when I thought about it. This wasn't how the world was supposed to work. This was *unfair*. And when the song came out, and that closing coda/round kicked in…

> *Feed the world*
> *Let them know it's Christmas time*

Crappy synth bells and all, it would bring a lump to my throat, and I'd see those children, my age and younger, with flies in their face and no energy to move them, and I'd think *dying*, and I'd think *starving to death*, and I'd be crying, unable to understand why the singers in the video smiled, why they weren't crying just thinking about it, how it was that life went on and we all went back to schools and work and reading and TV and eating and drinking and presents and Santa and these children couldn't move and were dying because they had no water and no food. I'd be choked up with useless tears, like I am now, writing this.

And please don't give me teach a man to fish. I mean, yes, obviously. Trivially. But fundamentally, feed the fucking starving children, okay?

And when they're all fed, with access to safe, clean water and roofs over their heads and clothes on their backs, by all means follow up with a hundredweight of rods and reels and seven million copies of *Fly Fishing* by JR Hartley translated into Ethiopian.

> *And the Christmas bells that are ringing*
> *Are the clanging bells of doom*

And hearing it now it's embarrassing for at least

two reasons, starting with white person guilt, land-of-not-just-plenty-but-excess guilt, and over-generalising bullshit. Do you have any idea how big Africa is, how diverse? Well, probably *you* do, because you're clearly the kind of educated, sensible person that only reads the finest collections of single author essays concerning childhood horrors, but I mean in a general sense—no snow in Africa? Really? Not even on the mountains? The Christian population doesn't know it's Christmas? Ever heard of the rainforest? Clue's in the fucking name. No, it's shameful, it is—it's the worst kind of well meaning yet paternalistic, over-sentimentalised, over-simplified sop whose sole purpose is to emotionally blackmail your cash from your wallet and into the charity tin. The chuggers outside Sainsbury's have more integrity, and more dignity. It's fucking shameless, and crass, and gross.

Also... life does go on. We absorb these human and inhumane horrors through our eyes and ears, take in the fact of child misery and starvation and death, and feel bad, and say things like 'fucking hell' and 'it's just horrible,' and we do, we feel bad, maybe hug our own kids a little tighter come bedtime, or text 'FOOD' or 'WATER' to the number that flashes on screen, or both. Then somehow, we go to bed and go to sleep and get up and go to work and max out our credit cards on plastic landfill for kids who'd rather have the cardboard box to play with half the time, and because the starving dying children aren't in our faces that very second, forget, and live in not just comfort but extreme excess.

Like it's not even happening.

And when I say *we*, I mean *me* first and foremost, to be clear. Of sinners I am the chief. I'll sometimes feel bad for a whole fifteen minutes before turning on *Breaking Bad* or *Justified* or *Hannibal*, and any sleepless nights I suffer won't have much to do with any of this stuff. And for all that I'm giving Geldof and Bono *et al* shit for crimes against songwriting, they have, in an immediate and material way, done more to help these people than I will in a hundred lifetimes. I speak not so much from the moral high ground as a deep and muddy ditch.

I don't do anything useful.

And somehow, we've convinced ourselves this is healthy, even normal—that the weird people are the over-sensitive souls who get so upset they can't function thinking about it, who become miserable and depressed and sometimes even suicidal because the obscene imbalance is too much, the naked greed alongside the desperate need just too dissonant and jagged for the conscience to take lined up so neatly. *They're* the ones who need medicating. *We're* normal, because we can just make ourselves indifferent to suffering, so long as we don't have to look at it or think about why it's happening.

I know all that now.

But I was six. And to a six-year-old, the song spoke perfectly to the feeling of what was going on. The futility. The awful juxtaposition of my life and the life of those children.

The horror.

And right smack in the middle, the line so dark, and true, and problematic, that they cut it from the latest release, even though Ebola should be scarier,

FEED THE WORLD

from a cynical point of view—after all, it's not like starvation is contagious (well, at least, not until the climate holocaust kicks in). If ever a dark and unworthy prayer was needed, it's in the face of a disease like this.

But even Bono has lost his stomach for this one, it seems. Which I think is a great pity.

Because sometimes even the crassest and most emotionally manipulative disposable pop art can speak to a deeper, darker truth. Can ring true with a statement, a sentiment, that shames us with its honesty, its raw and inherent hypocrisy, and which is really the only statement that's come close to explaining that 'it's complicated' bullshit masquerading as an answer, while the butter mountain melted and the grain mountain rotted and the people of Ethiopia faced mass extinction for lack of clean water and food. A statement that reveals far more than it intends, and little of it to our collective credit, but is undeniably genuine.

Well tonight thank God it's them
Instead of you.

SICKNESS WILL SURELY TAKE THE MIND

Tommy

I am in my Grandmother's house, with my sister, my Grandma, and my mother. Due to a combination of dull-even-to-me biographical facts surrounding the occasion, including which house Grandma is living in and who else is at the house, I can peg my age precisely to seven.

I am also, as I think on it, almost certainly unhappy, in a general sense. Having spent my childhood—my life, to this point, at least as far as remembered existence goes—in a rural setting (by which I mean the nearest village was a four mile walk and we didn't have a car, so, you know, pretty fucking rural) I'd recently been transplanted to a large, just-beginning-to-slip-into-post-industrial town in the north of England, and basically, I hated everything about it. A combination of my haircut and accent made me stick out a mile, rendering friendships conditional and one sided, always carrying a vague undertone of pity or charity. And going from twenty kids in your classroom to two hundred kids in your year was… well, disorientating is an understatement. I remember the sheer noise of the playground feeling like a physical assault, and the scale of the school canteen, with attendant sounds and smells, frequently induced nausea. Add in being one of the shortest kids in the year, and having a natural inclination to impress teachers, and it was never going to be a smooth transition.

It is also an obviously false but nonetheless crystal clear, insistent memory that everything and everyone smelled vaguely of stale chip fat.

It occurs to me now that one of the surest signs I'm unlikely to get on with another adult, to this day, is if they happen to say of their time in school, 'oh, but/and it was the best days of my life.'

Fuck off.

Anyway.

So I am—precisely—seven years old. And we're at the portion of the evening universally known as 'T.V. Time.' Grandma and mum are channel hopping, and my sister and I are pretending not to be tired, and also trying to be invisible—TV time at Grandma's house typically rendering bedtime an elastic concept, especially if we can avoid the temptation to argue with each other about, well, everything.

And channel hopping circa 1986 in the United Kingdom is a hilariously sparse affair, given that there are precisely four channels on offer. My memory is that it was BBC Two that gained my mother's delighted attention.

'Oh, look, The Who! I like The Who. Let's watch this!'

Sure, mum. Okay. Why not?

And the thing is, it's freaky from the get-go. Before a single overtly horrific thing has happened on camera, the experience is deeply disorienting. Everything's... off. I mean, there's the obvious thing, which is that nobody talks. All spoken communication is via song. And I must have seen musicals, but there's a step change difference between that and... this. Also, well, the horror isn't slow in coming. By the end of the opening song, Tommy is born on VE day, but his dad has already (apparently) died, our last sight of him burning in his plane as it plunges towards the earth. World War Two was still enough of an all-encompassing national mythology in '86 that as a seven-year-old, I could engage with the iconography—the flag waving, the nurses uniforms, the gas masks on the school kids. Who needs Moffatt?

So already, the prickly heat from Grandma's gas fire feels uncomfortable—no longer the soothing soporific, increasingly like the early onset of a fever. And when Oliver Reed slimes into frame as Uncle Frank (and was that a deep cut reference by Clive Barker, I find myself asking, at thirty one years remove?), the discomfort kicks up by an order of magnitude.

He's scary. I can't tell why, exactly, but he is. He drinks. He's sweaty. The way he acts towards Tommy's mum, something about it is badly wrong, and she seems oblivious, like a princess under a spell. The whole camp is deranged, an off-centre energy and cheer that's scary, like a place where terrible things would happen if your smile wasn't wide enough, and when Uncle Frank is taken back with Tommy, it feels like they've taken the madness home with them, invited it into their lives. When his mother asks Tommy if he likes Uncle Frank, and he replies sleepily, 'He's very nice, I think…'—I want to shout at them both.

And then, Tommy's real dad comes home.

This, I remember vividly. He visits Tommy's room first, looking on his son's sleeping form, his face scarred from the fire. Then he leaves. The music goes wild—crashing, clattering drums, keyboards, guitars, Tommy's father, shouting, his mother, sweating, crying, also shouting soundlessly, Tommy leaving his room, walking down the hall, my heart is pounding along with the maniac drums; don't go, kid, don't look, don't see, and Frank snarls, reaches for the lamp, Tommy throws the door open as his father is struck and crumples to the floor.

I mean, fucking hell.

His mother screams, bedsheets pressed to her naked body, 'What about the boy? He saw it all!'

They fall to their knees before him, talking, imploring, demanding. 'You didn't see it. You didn't hear it. You won't say anything, to anyone, ever.' It's an incantation, a spell, a curse. Their faces scared, angry, pleading, threatening, the music building to a crescendo, and as it breaks, Tommy looks into the camera, and there's a moment of movement, as though some door inside him has slammed shut.

'Now he is deaf. Now he is dumb. Now he is blind.'

His mother and Frank lead him down a corridor, a brick tunnel, endless. Lit from overhead. Like a prison. Like a dungeon. As the overture is played, he's taken to a funfair, an arcade, we see this kid sat in a waltzer, on a ferris wheel, in a hall of mirrors.

He is vacant, and the camera swirls and dives around him, lights swirling in and out of frame. Dissolves, wipes, as the music plays:

> *Sickness will surely take the mind, where minds don't usually go.*

Sickness of the mind. Not an alien concept, thanks to Floyd's *Dark Side Of The Moon*, but all the same, a deeply unsettling concept, one made worse by the fluid, queasy imagery and the knowledge that this sickness was not organic but inflicted.

Damage.

And really, it should have ended there. It was past my bedtime. But that was the very definition of a double-edged statement, wasn't it? Because this was The Forbidden Time. I wanted to stay up.

And to stay up meant to see.

And so it went.

Christmas. Tommy sat in a toy car, hugely expensive. Staring into space. The other children encircling, blowing horns he can't hear in his face, taunting. His mother's pleading, Frank angry (of course), the fear for Tommy's soul, and the moment he smashes the baby Jesus toy into the manger scene. I remember thinking, poor kid.

Crossfade, and the child is an adult, still staring into space. He's in a church, but again, something is wrong. The preacher is playing a guitar, and the altar boys are musicians with wild eyes and long hair. The song goes on and on, an ode to the healing power of The Woman. A huge statue is brought down the aisle, the goddess in a frilly dress. The congregation file

SICKNESS WILL SURELY TAKE THE MIND

past her, touching the hem of her dress, kissing her feet. Those in wheelchairs are pushed past, their helpers touching the statue and transferring that touch to their heads. Finally, the church is empty. Tommy's mother takes him forward, but he does not want to kneel, to kiss the feet, and she pushes his head down, he resists, and in the struggle, the statue tips, falls, and breaks.

Her face fractures into three pieces. I remember feeling horrified by that, without knowing why.

Then, oh shit.

So, Uncle Frank takes Tommy to... A place. A room. A girl. She claims that she can cure him. She just needs one night. She's the Gypsy. The Acid Queen.

As soon as Frank leaves, she produces a syringe full of a bright red liquid.

If I'd had a sofa to hide behind, this would have been the moment.

Instead, I watch as she places Tommy in a giant metal suit covered in needles. The suit closes on him, puncturing him, my mind assures me, in several places, and then all the syringes on the outside fill with the red liquid, before the plungers depress, sending it into his bloodstream. Also, the silver device starts to rotate. The music goes mental again, the song crashes around, the thing spins faster and faster while the woman wails and laughs, and then it slows, and I don't want it to, and it stops, and I don't want it to, and it slowly opens, and inside is a skeleton with snakes crawling over its bones, silver ball bearings pouring out on the floor.

It closes. It spins. It slows. It opens again. This

time, Tommy has a crown of poppies. Also poppies covering each puncture wound, though blood helpfully trickles down his limbs, to remind you of what lies beneath. At some point, he also turns into his father. At some point the spinning contraption shrinks until it enters the acid queen's mouth.

At some point, roughly 4.7 billion years later, Frank comes in, and takes Tommy home in disgust.

Time to get off? Fuck, yes. Way past time.

But then, I've come this far. It's late.

'Do you think it's all right? To leave the boy with cousin Kevin? Do you think it's all right? There's something about him I don't really like. Do you think it's all right?'

'I think it's all right, yes I think it's all right.'

It fucking is not all right.

Cousin Kevin plays the piano, lamenting his lack of a play friend, and then opines that there's a lot he can do with a freak. Before slamming a paper bag over Tommy's head.

And then it's just an express elevator to hell.

He's the school bully. And his victim can't speak. Can't fight back. Tommy has a cigarette put out on his arm. He is held down in a full bathtub, then hung from the door by his collar and whipped. There are six inch nails sticking up through his toilet seat, and glass in his dinner.

And I have fucking had enough.

I protest. Loudly. Mum turns over. Reluctantly.

She flips back, briefly, after a short interval—'I'm sure it'll have finished now'—and I see Tommy pushed down a flight of spiral stairs.

She tunes away again. But she's not done. And as

she tunes back, and Tommy is ironed dry by cousin Kevin, she assures me, it's all over, the scary bit has finished, and isn't the music good?

I couldn't tell you how I responded.

Anyway, Tommy is taken home. Cleaned up.

And then they need another sitter.

'Do you think it's all right…'

Fucking no!

And of course, it's Uncle Ernie.

And roughly two nanoseconds after he cracks a raw egg into a pint of ale and downs it before pulling on sweaty red rubber gloves, I am done.

This time, there is no protest, or attempt to turn it back over.

And, you know, when I finally got to finish the movie (not at fifteen, or nineteen, both of which I had to abort at the same point, unable to make it past Uncle Ernie and his heavy breathing, but finally in my late twenties), it turned out that I'd bailed at pretty much the moment of maximum discomfort. From that point, the narrative turns, with Tommy's discovery of pinball and eventual cure, and while you couldn't fairly call it a happy ending, it's never quite as bleak, as menacing, as fever-dream terrifying as the moment his parents walk out of the room and leave young Tommy alone with wicked Uncle Ernie.

But as a kid, I couldn't know that. So I bailed, and left Tommy in that room. And I think somehow, in my mind, because of that, Tommy is always in that room—trapped within himself, helpless, at the mercy of a horror of a man, a creature without empathy, only dark appetites.

And part of me is trapped in there with him.

IT IS YOUR FAVOURITE PLANET, AFTER ALL

Doctor Who and the Terror of the Autons

I am between eight and ten years old. I can be no more precise. I can only be even that precise because I remember the school, and the village the school was in.

Crappy fucking village. *Creepy* fucking village. Creepy as hell. Every bonfire night, there would be a torch lit procession from the church to the huge pile of wood in the village square. Everyone would be there. The vicar up front, alongside the bigger farmers, the shop and garage owners, the chamber of commerce types, then the regular village folk. Everyone.

In the centre of the bonfire was a stake. Big enough for... well, a person. It was always empty. Never a Guy. Somehow, that was the worst thing about it, to me. That empty space. It was threatening. A statement. Yeah, it's empty... this year...

Our tiny house was next to a pub. One evening at kicking out time, there was some kind of disturbance—not sure if a window got broken or it was just pebbles, but something. When the local constabulary came round the next day for my mum to file a report, he took a look around the house while my sister and I (seven and nine, probably) huddled at the top of the stairs, then looked my mother in the eye and said, 'Well, madam, you *do* have a Greenpeace sticker in your window.'

Two years, we lived there.

The school... man, where to start? Outside toilets, in a building that resembled a shed. I mean, indoor ones too, to be fair, but still. An outdoor section of the playing field that was corrugated off, and contained to my initial delight and subsequent dumb horror an outdoor swimming pool; a one hundred per cent unheated, bug filled, arctic plague pit, that I am sure will one day be responsible for developing the world's first sentient verruca. Though as I cast my mind back to some of the 'children' I somehow survived being cooped up with, I can't dismiss the possibility that had already happened, and I was just too busy trying to avoid being beaten up to notice.

I tell you something, too, I know there's been various attempts at anti-bullying approaches through the decades, and each has its pros and cons, unintended consequences, and the last thing I'd do is dismiss anybody else's experienced misery on the subject, because God fucking knows if you've been there, it's shit. But I will say: I doubt like hell there's too many schools left whose anti-bullying policy could be summed up with the phrase, 'Well, he's moving up next year.'

That was it, by the way. I guess the 'try and keep out of his way' was implied, albeit laughable in a school with a total population across the infants and juniors (two classes, separated by a decidedly non-soundproof foldaway 'wall') of *maybe* sixty kids. In

MY LIFE IN HORROR VOLUME I

practical terms, you might as well say 'try and be invisible,' to which my response would probably have been, 'I *am* fucking trying!'

As things turned out, there were worse kids, and I wouldn't leave the building for good without throwing my first punch in anger. Still, even before, I wasn't having fun.

The one 'out' was Friday afternoons. That was when the headmaster and our teacher, no doubt exhausted after his long week of solid 9am to 3:10pm not-giving-a-single-solitary-shit, would finally abandon all pretence at running an institution of learning and set us free within the classroom to do as we liked.

In my case, that meant the library corner.

This was a single wall mounted white wire rack in the corner of the classroom, stocked by the mobile North Devon County Council library service every month or so. A rotating cast of paperbacks encased in clear plastic, with white borrowing slips stuck over the first page, often obscuring the inside blurb or press. It was a meagre selection, with one crucial saving grace—there would always be at least one or two Target *Doctor Who* books.

Here's the weird part: I can't remember a time when I didn't know *Doctor Who*. I am literally unable to remember a time when *Doctor Who* wasn't a part of my internal imaginative landscape; a time when the Doctor wasn't part of my personal pantheon of heroes—every bit as vital and immortal as Indy or Luke Skywalker, and English, to boot. In fact, even that understates it: I remember seeing *Jedi* in the cinema at five, *Temple Of Doom*, as discussed,

IT IS YOUR FAVOURITE PLANET, AFTER ALL

at six. But the Doctor? He's just always been there, him and the wheezing, groaning sound that heralds the arrival of a blue Police box and the promise that shit is about to get off the hook bonkers.

And the reason that's odd is that I didn't have a television in my house until 1986, by which time I was seven.

I remember that, you can bet. *Trial of a Timelord*, Colin Baker... I sometimes think one of the big reasons I don't find Colin Baker as obnoxious as so many others is because I first saw him in black and white. Shorn of the constant mental irritation of that fucking outfit, there is stuff to like about his performance, I think. And anyway, he was my first.

Except that can't be right either, because he wasn't. I knew all about *Doctor Who*, and Daleks, and Cybermen and Autons and The Master and the TARDIS and K-9, sonic screwdrivers, Sarah and Harry and Barbara and Ian and all of it, for years before The Valyard tried to send my hero down in glorious monochrome over the autumn of 1986.

So it had to be the Target paperbacks.

And I mean, duh, right? I learned to read before I got to school, thanks to the extraordinary patience of my mum, and I still remember with clarity the day I discovered/ was taught reading in my head.... woosh! I was five. So that, plus school libraries, plus no TV yet, and nonetheless still containing a head teeming with extensive *Who* lore, equals Target.

Specifically, Terrance Dicks.

And *Terror of the Autons* I remember especially well.

There are a few reasons for that, but chief has to

be the cover. Which is a thing of twisted beauty that you really should Google image search right now. Go ahead. I'll wait.

Now admittedly, the squid/eyeball/tentacle critter barely features in the story, but if one look at that cover doesn't make you want to pull this book off the shelf and commence devouring it, just know that you and seven-year-old me will never be friends.

But there's more to it than that. Rereading the story for this essay, I was astonished at just how much of it I'd internalised, in terms of the shape and flow of the plot, the big moments, even much of The Master's dialogue. Reading it was a profoundly odd experience, because I kept getting this powerful doubling effect, like I was reading the words *before* reading them. It's like the damn thing has been photocopied up there or something. And I mean, sure, part of that is just the age I was at the time, and that old word 'impressionable' has rarely felt more apt, but...

...well, look, I sat in that library corner and read every day for two years. And I can remember hardly any of what I read back then, even the *Doctor Who*. So why this one? Why was it that as soon as the idea for this essay series came up, I knew with a moral certainty that I'd end up writing about *Doctor Who and the Terror of the Autons*, sooner or later?

Well, first, because Terrance Dicks, obviously. The man has been described elsewhere as having a prose style that is 'ruthlessly efficient' and I certainly can't argue with that. But the reread showed me more—or at least, showed me *why* that's such a powerful tool.

IT IS YOUR FAVOURITE PLANET, AFTER ALL

He manages to create these amazing bit part players with an incredible level of interiority in just a few short sentences. There's Luigi Rossini (born Lew Ross, in Hoxton, a fact we learn in the opening paragraph of the book)—owner of a shabby circus that employs desperate performers on their way out (or in trouble), and pays starvation wages. Within two paragraphs, we know him, understand him, and intensely dislike him. In a similar word count, later, we're introduced to Albert Goodge, an aging scientist working at the deep space radio telescope whose obsession with the poor quality of the packed lunch his wife provides manages to be funny and somehow faintly poignant at once.

And that's just the background characters—the poor unfortunates who have managed to find themselves in a *Doctor Who* story without realising it, and are therefore doomed. When the time comes to meet the main cast—Joe, The Brig, Yates, the Doctor—they leap off the page and take up residence in your skull, like the ghosts of departed but well remembered friends. It's astonishing.

And then, of course, there is the story. My understanding is that the Beeb got in some trouble for this one on broadcast from the blue rinse brigade, and based on this novelisation it's not hard to see why. The 'killer plastic' motif is exploited in a number of terrifying ways (which is how I get away with talking about *Doctor Who* in a collection of essays on horror influences, if you were wondering). Killer dolls, killer flowers that shoot suffocating film over your mouth and nose, killer furniture, for crying out loud. Not forgetting what must have been an iconic screen moment (so powerful it gets an illustration in the Target book) when the Doctor peels off the face of a policeman who is ostensibly rescuing him, only to find a faceless plastic dummy beneath, which, wow, just wow. It's pretty bloody thrilling in the book, if I'm honest. And sure, that's actually an idea from the mind of script writer Robert Holmes, bless his little cotton subversive no-authority-can-really-be-trusted socks, but the moment got my heart pounding as I read it, at seven and at thirty-seven, and that's at least partly down to Mr. Dicks not fucking it up in prose.

I could bang on all night—how long have you got? The Master is bloody brilliant in this one; could it really be his first story? Feels like he's always been part of the geography of the show. He's manipulative, suave, apparently perfectly buttoned down but of course seething with repressed rage, hypnotising away like a good'un. And his plan makes no sense at all unless viewed as basically screaming at the Doctor, 'Look at me and how clever I am!' via the medium of attempted homicide. Which, as new series aficionados will understand, is exactly how they ultimately explain all this wonderful glorious nonsense. The Auton concept is pushed in a ton of interesting and terrifying directions, using the classic *Doctor Who* trick of 'let's-make-an-everyday-household-object-a-source-of-terror' and taking it Tap-like all the way to eleven—I mean to say, anything plastic can kill you! On behalf of seven-year-old me, you bastards.

Also, thank you. Thank you so, so much. Because for a terrified, bullied, bright but alienated seven-year-old, who was awkward and did not fit in the environment he found himself, you provided… an escape. No, better, a portal into another world, another place. Yeah, okay… a TARDIS, if you want to be strictly accurate.

And sure, the world you took me to was scary. But, fuck, the world I was escaping was scary too. I had bullies and apathetic authority figures, and for that matter policemen who didn't give a shit. At least in *Doctor Who* they were controlled by an evil alien intelligence, which made some kind of sense.

And, in your world, there was the Doctor.

Sure, he's old, arrogant, kind of an asshole to his friends. Sure, he spends half his time trying to escape the planet, and he's impatient, and at times ridiculously overconfident. And yes, he leans on his charisma, uses it to breeze past all the above to make people like him and do what he wants. But he's the Doctor. He cares. He is righteous. He has zero tolerance for bullshit or macho posturing, he's empathetic, he's tenacious and angry and always the smartest person in the room. He dresses like an Australian's nightmare (for those of you keeping score, that's two Spinal Tap references so far), and disrespects authority every chance he gets, and the one thing he really, really cannot abide is cruelty.

The Doctor was my hero. Aw hell, why bother with the past tense pretence? The Doctor *is* my hero. He always will be. The hooks in my psyche run deep, too deep to extract even if I had the slightest desire, which I don't. Because when you're sat in the corner, surrounded by a world you cannot understand, full of banal evils and casual cruelties, the notion that out there, somewhere, is a man with a time machine who can travel anywhere and anywhen, getting into adventures and writing wrongs and standing up to and beating every bully in the universe... it almost makes all of it worthwhile.

No, scratch that. It *does* make it all worthwhile.

The notion that there's a better world, with, yes, villains and bullies and death, but also, crucially, heroes—smart, compassionate people for whom force is a last resort, and for whom intellect and empathy are always prized higher than brute strength and the ability to inflict harm. A universe where, yes, there are monsters, but also a man the monsters are afraid of. A man who bends his surroundings into a better place by force of will, who can stare every oppressor and false authority and demagogue in the eye and say, 'not good enough,' a man who cannot prevent horror, cannot stop death, a man who exists in a universe where bad things sometimes happen to good people, but who stands, who fights, who makes a difference. Who makes things better.

Even if it only exists as a story.

SOMEDAY, YOU MAY BE READY

Gremlins

Was I nine? Ten? Somewhere around there.

My dad had a robust approach to movies and age ratings—one somewhat at odds with his book policy (as noted above and below). While I could read pretty much whatever I liked, generally speaking, if the British Board of Film Classifications said it was only suitable for fifteen year olds and up, I was shit out of luck. Of course, if they said 'Parental Guidance' it was treated as good enough (hence the above encounter with a certain *Temple Of Doom*).

So it was a rare occasion indeed when my dad would say 'they got it wrong' and let my younger sister and I watch a fifteen, and for that reason, such occasions were moments of deep celebration for us.

This movie was one of those times.

Our excitement was palpable. For starters, we had the VHS on a 48-hour rental, so we could watch it multiple times (I think we got to twelve viewings). The cover looked exciting—just a box with a pair of eyes, and *that* lettering for the movie name. Dad was working during the day—must have been a half term break—and Grandma was babysitting, so basically, it was all our TV, all the time. And, you know, it was a fifteen! Thrilling beyond words. The anticipation was almost unbearable, expectations sky high.

Gremlins exceeded them with room to spare.

We were hooked from the opening. I'm sure under the harsh light of today's more savvy and racially sensitive audiences, the opening sequence with an elderly Chinese gentlemen shopkeeper is at least a bit uncomfortable (especially the 'Dragon breath' gag), but as a couple of yokel children from whitebread North Devon, that sailed over our heads—all we cared about was that creature.

Gizmo has to be one of the great achievements of physical effects in cinema. In fact, I'd put him up there with 30s King Kong and Carpenter's *The Thing*. No, really.

He's perfect.

The big eyes, the gentle, nervous smile, the plush hair—there's not a child alive who didn't see that movie and immediately say, 'I want one!' I'll never know how Furby escaped a lawsuit from the creators of Gizmo—because, come on.

More importantly, he's a character—a central one. I mean, in plot terms, he isn't - in raw story terms, he's the McGuffin - but what genius it was to decide to imbue the source of such chaos and mayhem with a cute face and lovable personality. My sister and I fell in love, the way children do, and like all such childhood loves, it's never entirely left me. If the film were made today, no doubt we'd all rhapsodise about how amazing the CGI fur was, and what a great job Andy Serkis did with the facial expression work. But this was done the old fashioned way—with physical props and a lot of elbow grease, along with some superlative shooting and editing. It's wonderful.

I remember the pacing being superb, too—the

story unrolls, all the events logically following, enough time spent with each change to assimilate it, without ever dragging. It seems effortless, and I'm amazed how few modern movies manage it—they're all either cut like MTV videos, to the point of confusion if not incoherence, or tedious slogs through 'worthy' periods of history.

Wow. This essay from *My Life In Horror* brought to you in association with ten-year-old me, grumpy old man me, and the 'Get Off My Lawn' school of film criticism. I blame the Irish whisky.

Anyway.

Point is, this film is a majestic piece of storytelling, beautifully plotted and paced. And the effects are outstanding. I have vivid memories of replaying the microwave scene and the blender scene over and over again, even using frame advance to enjoy the exploding Gremlin head in all its dark green glory. Similarly, the birth of the 'problem' Mogwai(s?), the hatching of the Gremlins, Stripe in the pool… in fact, if you can think of an effect sequence in that film, you can guarantee that I've watched it at two frames per second, slack jawed with amazement at the awesomeness of it all.

It's also hilarious. Like the way The Garbage Pail Kids was hilarious, which is to say gross, if not grotesque. And it was scary at the same time. Take the death of the old lady on the stair lift. Yes, she was an irredeemably unpleasant character, but her fate is pretty nasty—stair lift rewired such that she's fired like a missile out of her upstairs window and into the street. The first time I watched it was in stunned silence.

The second time, I could barely breathe for laughing.

I'm sure that's an artefact of seeing it as a young kid—and probably a young, sheltered kid at that. *Temple* aside, I hadn't been exposed to much, if any, cinematic horror at this point in my life, and *Gremlins* is, at least in terms of plot structure, a horror movie. Nonetheless, I remember the pattern clearly—first time through, the whole film was heart-in-my-mouth from start to finish, with subsequent viewings being an experience so different as to be almost unrecognisable—namely in a state of perpetual giggles.

I was far too young to have the words for any of this stuff, or understand why it was so good or worked on both levels. Plus, I'm just a gullible consumer of movies, I guess, in the sense that I'm easily seduced by the notion of horror. Like, I saw *Arachnophobia* when I was a mid-teenager, and thought *that* was a horror movie first time through—and not because I'm scared of spiders either (because I ain't). But I *experienced* it. I lived it. I got it on an instinctive, gut level, because when you make a good enough feature, people don't need to get film theory or narrative complexity to be blown away. It just happens because you made a fucking awesome movie.

But I'm grateful I was that young, that naive, that innocent, even. I learned so much about horror storytelling from getting to see the movie in that way. It freaked me the hell out, a bunch of times. The moment when the record starts playing in the empty house. The howling noise and smoke as the cocoons hatch. Actually, the appearance of the cocoons—gross, dark, alien. The death of the school science teacher is a masterful piece of suspense cinema, a near perfect 'I-know-you're-going-to-try-and-make-me-jump-but-oh-you-bastard-you-*still*-got-me' scene.

And oh, Stripe! Stripe with saw blades. Stripe with a chainsaw. He's such a great villain, is Stripe. Every bit as much a character as Gizmo, with all the cute inverted into vicious violence and sadism with a smile. The Gremlin creature design is superlative, and Stripe as the poster boy is magnificent. The bastard is so scary he even manages to land a post-death jump scare.

Sure, even the first time, the Gremlin group scenes are funny—in the bar and the cinema. But in the bar, well, Kate is stuck in there with them and that looks like no fun at all, and of course, in the cinema, our heroes getting detected flips the mood on a dime from hilarity to pulse pounding fear. Even in those outright broad comedic moments, there's a tense, stressful undertone—at least there was for me, age ten, desperately afraid for Billy and Kate and Gizmo.

Many, many years later, I'd learn this lesson again, with movies like *Pulp Fiction* and *Fight Club* (and of course, as discussed above, *RoboCop*). But I think *Gremlins* was the first time a movie became a fundamentally different viewing experience the second time from the first, and the reason for that is, for all the sight gags and absurdity of the situation, *Gremlins* is, in structure, pacing, and bricks-and-mortar storytelling, a horror movie.

MY LIFE IN HORROR VOLUME I

The two days flew by, and my sister and I talked about it for months, years afterwards. The DVD still holds a pride of place on my movie shelf. I genuinely hadn't thought about it until I sat to write this—I'd remembered the laughs, the rewatches—but *Gremlins* was as formative a horror movie experience for me as *Jaws* or *The Thing*.

Thank you, Joe Dante, for the horror and the wonder. For terrorising a ten-year-old kid.

And second time through, for the laughs too.

OLD MAN, WHY DO YOU SMOKE?

Scott (Absent Friends 1)

This essay was originally written in 2012, as part of an attempt to drive traffic to the short-lived, now defunct website of my rather longer lived but also now defunct band, The Disciples Of Gonzo. I think this neatly exemplifies the depth of my understanding of what makes for good cross marketing and a coherent approach to creative output (as personified by, well, this book).

It is also one of the best and most personal things I've ever written.

On Friday, while I was at a gig, my sister phoned the house and left a message with Mrs. Gonzo for me, which I got on Saturday morning. The message was both a bolt from the blue and utterly unsurprising.

Scott died.

This is not the first time someone has given me this news, actually. When I was nineteen, Scott's then-ex-drummer and my then-future-ex-psychotic-housemate Steve told me he'd died—apparently, he'd been hanging out with a group of travellers, ripped off all their money and spent it on heroin, and they'd beaten him to death. You're just going to have to trust me when I tell you that it says more about Scott and less about my gullibility that I believed this for a few months; at least until another good friend of the time, Luke, put me straight, having seen Scott over the summer (Scott's quote to Luke was very Scott—'If Steve doesn't stop telling stories about me, big people are going to come and sit in his garden').

At the time I was told that, I thought he was the first person my age that I'd personally known who died, and it made me miserable (not to mention engendering a feeling of foreboding about my own future, and the future in general—I could be quite histrionic in those days, believe it or not). In the event, that dubious honour went to a guy called Kye, who deserves his own piece, and who most assuredly didn't die of a drug overdose or related shenanigans.

So who is... sorry, was... Scott?

I've been thinking about this quite a bit over the last 48 hours, and I've discovered to my dismay that he was quite a bit more important to me than I'd appreciated when he was alive. For example, although I always think of myself as someone who is more comfortable with women than men, I've been extremely fortunate to have a series of intense, platonic but deep relationships with men over the years—normally though not always rooted in a shared passion for either music or politics, plus humor. In school there was James, college Chris (that didn't end well) and later Rob (still going strong), through Live Action Role Playing I met Nate (no man can make me laugh as hard or as long), and later at work, Adrian, and still later, at my current place of employment, Brett (in between there was London, with Ian, Andy, and the whole tabletop RPG gang).

OLD MAN, WHY DO YOU SMOKE?

For a while at school, I thought Scott was one of those. He wasn't, as it turned out, and I learned a valuable life lesson about the dangers of trusting charismatic people, and for that matter of mistaking charisma for sincerity. Scott wasn't the last time I got burned that way (see Chris, as mentioned earlier), but I definitely got better at spotting such personality types as a result, as well as devising strategies for how to protect myself (basically, in my case, saying goodbye, and meaning it).

More on that later.

I first met Scott when I was ten, and he was eleven. I know this because of where I met him—at the Plough Arts centre youth drama club. I could, and perhaps should, do an entire essay on just this place (*and, indeed, I since have, but you'll have to wait until* Volume II *to read it)*, given that it gave me my first taste of the performance drug that is still such an integral part of my personality and drive. For now, just know that it was an amazing service provided by unbelievably talented and dedicated people, and a ray of sunshine for a shit-ton of kids in otherwise pretty unremarkable and often pretty crappy circumstances.

And it's where I met Scott, and I fell pretty hard.

Scott had effortless charisma. You just wanted to look at him, and listen to him. He was also smart, and funny, and just So Damn Cool. He really was, even at eleven. He knew it too (or at least definitely did later), but he wore it lightly, and enjoyed other people. I remember getting an incredible buzz out of making him laugh—I figured it meant more if coming from someone who could be so funny. Plus, he was one of those people who you wanted to like you.

The two main identifiable social groups during my childhood were Townies and Goths—even though almost none of the Goths listened to Goth music—that's North Devon for you. And the thing is, Scott was never a Townie, but even the Townies knew he was cool, so Goths who could count Scott as a friend could also count on a little less flack from Townies, at least while he was about. I remember being excited at the prospect that Scott would be in the same year as me when I went to Secondary School, and bitterly disappointed when we were placed in different forms (though it's as well for my grades that we were, I suspect).

For a little while there, I imagined he was my best friend. I invited him to my birthday do when I was—shit, eleven, twelve, surely no older. One of my other friends, John (who would later also call himself Scott's best friend, and get similarly burned) had taken me out on his birthday to Westward Ho! arcades, where we fed I-don't-know-how-much money into arcade machines, for hours. A video game junkie even then, it was one of my best days out ever, and I wanted to do the same thing with Scott (poor old John didn't get a look in—it's interesting that it's only now, reflecting on this at twenty-two years distance, that I feel guilt and embarrassment).

Of course, we couldn't go to Westward Ho!, and we didn't have anything like the money that John's parents had, so we went to Exeter and the arcade there and spent £10 each, and by the end of it I remember having that faint and sick feeling in my stomach that I'd wasted money. Knowing how little money we had, this was a horrible experience. And Scott acted up terribly—he could drink milk through his nose, and demonstrated this in the car to my horrified and fascinated sister, and just plain horrified mum. I remember him making a paper airplane and trapping it in the window of our moving car so the wing would flap on the outside, and I'm sure if you asked my mum she could give you chapter and verse on Scott's bad behavior that day—I was certainly told in clear terms that he would not be invited to any such future events. Not that this had much of a dampening effect on my hero worship of the guy.

We started learning guitar at the same time, but he had an *electric* guitar, an imitation Gibson, which given we were both rabid Guns N' Roses fans (it being 1989, with *Use Your Illusion* still two years away, and *Appetite For Destruction* riding high as the best fucking album in existence) meant he was a million times cooler. Besides, I wanted to be a singer, and he was only one of a million who thought that wasn't a good idea; to be fair, hearing a prepubescent voice trying to sing the Axl whine was probably at best a touch unsettling. I remember one long coach trip (thinking back on my school career, this will have been the only time I was cool enough to sit right at the back until my fifth year—such was the aura Scott carried), sharing a walkman, one earbud each, me trying to sing along to *Appetite* and *Skid Row*, and him hitting me over the head with a rolled up magazine each time I messed up or made up a word—which was a lot. It should tell you something about how I felt about him that this still qualifies as a happy memory, despite it sounding a bit mean in black and white.

Such is the power of love, or hero worship.

I have other, disjointed memories of Scott from this time. He'd claimed to have seen the *Nightmare on Elm Street* movies, including the then-just-released fifth movie *The Dream Child*, and invented some outrageous and disturbing lies about its content.

He also told me he was going to take me to see Guns N' Roses supporting The Rolling Stones, and man, I told everyone about that, and was excited for months, before he told me I couldn't go because one of his uncles six Harleys had broken down and the other five rides were already accounted for. He made some vague promise about Iron Maiden the following February, which I told people about as a face-saver, but I never got over that disappointment (and if you were eleven and Guns N' Roses were your gateway to a lifetime of obsession with all things rock, I imagine you wouldn't have either).

We saw each other less, and he hooked up with a new best friend. He also started getting into The Wonderstuff, Carter USM, The Levellers, and other music I dismissed as 'crusty' i.e. not rock enough—though Nirvana, I had to admit, were pretty good. I remember vividly—God, it's so funny how this stuff comes back—on a school coach trip when we were all fifteen or so, a Blur song came on the radio (is it called 'There's no other way'?—I'm too lazy to look it up) and all the Townies sang along, and Scott turned to his best friend, and they both looked horrified, genuinely upset, and I remember Scott saying, really sadly, 'don't worry man—we heard it first!' I also remember telling him about *Use Your*

Illusion—by '91 he wouldn't even admit to knowing who GnR were, let alone drop actual money on an album—and seeing him interested, but in a purely academic way, so removed from the shared passion of a few years before. I couldn't understand what had changed, but something clearly had, and that old GnR magic was just dead to him.

I guess, in the interest of full disclosure, I should also mention that he went out for a while with the girl I spent the entirety of secondary school with a massive and unrequited crush on; any of us can look back and laugh at that shit now, and we should, but at the time it was total fucking agony, and I was happy beyond words when it ended. Worst week of my life.

Then again, he was still the coolest motherfucker in school. Example: Chris (different Chris), a large and arrogant and deeply stupid bully and bad boy of some repute had said something Scott didn't like—I want to say it was a slight on Scott's father who died, but actually I think it was less emotive, something more where Chris had called Scott a liar about something. Anyway, they had a fight, but it was a weird fight—they set a date, time (lunch break) and venue (my form room, which was a treat). The fighters assembled, there was a big assed crowd, and the desks were cleared to form an arena in the middle of the floor. I mean, they took it pretty fucking seriously. And I learned a thing or two about bullies that day too, because Chris, the big hard man about school, was just about shitting himself before Scott even got into the room. He just kept saying, 'I'm going to lose, man,' over and over, with a scared smile I think I'd never seen to that point.

Needless to say, he was right, and Scott hurt him bad enough to make him cry and issue a very full public apology. Scott never got much shit from the bullies before that (he was a big, solid kid) but he got zero from that day, and even though we weren't close anymore by then, I felt that old pull of hero worship—after all, he'd done what I never would, was not capable of—he'd stood up, hit back, and won respect in the only language those assholes ever understood. He beat them on their terms.

I mean, seriously, how fucking cool could one guy be?

He formed a band while still at secondary school (and we didn't have a sixth form, so he was certainly under sixteen)—The Push, I think. They even had John of the aforementioned best birthday ever (and by then Scott's new, new best friend) who played tambourine and danced—so I guess Scott had heard and seen Happy Mondays by then. I don't know how many shows they played, or what they sounded like—except that's bullshit, because I knew they sounded good, and my bitterness and inadequacies could absolutely not handle seeing them confirm it. I don't know if this makes sense, but to me, having grown up with and been the same age as this kid, and loving Rock every bit as much, albeit in now divergent styles, to see him up there doing it would just corroborate my failures, and I honestly couldn't handle that emotionally. Looking back, that is a real regret, and clearly not to my credit. I remember talking to Scott about some of his songs—one memory is of him recounting his embarrassment about an anti-smoking song he'd written when he was 'younger'—he was maybe fourteen when he told me this—and looking at it now, what's the word for when irony becomes too painful to be funny?

> *Old man, why do you smoke?*
> *Old man, why do you choke?*

Damn, wish I'd heard it.

He also performed an anti-drug song (with new best friend on guitar) in a school assembly once, though the lyrics were very mumbled in delivery, and I got the indistinct impression it was a bit more equivocal in content than it'd been sold as being.

(Others did see The Push, and suggest I was right to be worried about how good they were. The aforementioned Luke, around the time he was helpfully debunking the first 'Scott is dead' rumour, told me, 'Man, The Push were great man, they really were. But Scott was just mental, you know, he always had that craziness. I remember one gig, he'd gotten there late and was either drunk or high, and he hadn't tuned his guitar, so he just got on stage and said, 'We're The Push, and we don't believe in tuning our instruments' and then just played the *whole fucking gig* out of tune. I mean, on the one hand, that's so rock 'n roll right? But on the other hand, it sounded fucking horrible! That's Scott, man.')

Scott could also punch pretty hard, and he was hypersensitive about being called a liar (a trait I have since observed in other charming liars I have known). One evening, on the school bus home, I made some comment about him lying about the Guns

N' Roses gig we never went to. We were both older then, me fifteen, him sixteen, and I'd seen GnR thanks to my father (and seriously, thanks Dad. Nine Inch Nails first UK show; Skid Row slagging off Brent council, and GnR performing for three hours at Wembley Stadium? Yeah, you know how to pick a good Rock Show, my man). Lord alone knows how Scott and I got into it that day. He was on the backseat, I was next from the back (year five, remember?) and I was sitting up and turned around talking to him, and somehow we got on the subject of the-gig-that-never-was, and I called him a liar, and he punched me in the eye, hard. He said words to the effect of, 'You deserved that.' I said, 'Why, because you're a liar?' He hit me again, hard, same spot. In the gap before the pain kicked in and I started crying, I said, 'You can hit me as many times as you want, Scott, it won't stop me saying it.' The fire went out of his eyes, and he spent the rest of the bus journey trying to justify what he'd done and explain why the show had never happened, and I tried (and, let's be honest, failed) to not cry.

None of this shit matters now—I want you to understand that. But, fuck me, it mattered then. Do we ever again feel things with the same intensity that we do at that age?

That week, I got my first and only award from the school's end of year prize giving, and I did it sporting a magnificent black eye, which had there been photos, might have been more embarrassing or cool. As it is, it's a story my mum loves to tell, so I thought I'd save you some time.

Scott apologized, as only Scott could—a few

weeks later, someone (it may have been John) presented me with a copy of AC/DC *Back in Black* on vinyl. Inside the sleeve (so I'd have to find it before playing the record) was a scrap of paper with the words 'an apology. Scott' written on it. At some point even later, I talked to Scott, and I remember saying, 'You didn't give Chris a record after you punched him, did you?' He grinned. 'Nah, Chris deserved it.'

As bad as I suspected things were getting with him, I felt a flash of that old love just then. I still have the record. The note, alas, is gone. Another regret. If I close my eyes, I can picture it still. His handwriting.

Scott got into drugs in a big way, as you've probably gathered. At his new, new best friend's sixteenth, which I was also invited to, I saw Scott under the influence of acid, something I'd never witnessed first hand. I watched him play with an invisible bouncy rubber ball, which he declared repeatedly to be the best in the world. He later told me that he'd lost two hours out of the day when he caught his reflection in the mirror, and watched his face change into, amongst other things, a wolf man, and something he called 'chessboard Tron man.' Also, a group of us were watching the film Critters late that evening, and there's a scene where an alien bounty hunter takes human form by creating a human body—skeleton, then blood, muscle, etc, in a stop-motion gore fest of a sequence. Scott walked in as it started and stood transfixed, jaw fully unhinged through the whole forty-five second sequence, before slowly turning to us and saying in a hushed voice, 'did that just happen?'

That's the last time I can remember seeing Scott, actually, prior to the actual last time, years later. I don't know if he went to college and dropped out or just didn't go, but he wasn't on the same bus as me anymore. John was, his new (new) best friend, and I remember he told me at one point that Scott had asked him for £120, and if he didn't get it, someone was going to break his legs. I remember John felt so horrible about it, because it was his best friend, but also a near impossible sum of money for a sixteen-year-old. I guess it's also testament to the lasting power of Scott's charm that it took me years to even suspect the threat to Scott might not have been real, and he may have just been trying to extort cash from John. Of course, it also could have been true. But I don't remember ever hearing he got his legs broken.

Actually, that reminds me of another Scott story—one day, at school, he'd either lost or not gotten his lunch money (and I'm pretty sure this was genuine). I saw him around 1pm (lunch was 12:30 – 1:30) and he told me the story and asked for 10p—I'm pretty sure I gave it—I know I would have done if I had it, and I probably did. Anyway, I remember leaving around 1:10, and seeing him sitting there, with a plate of chips, meat pie, dessert with pink custard and a 500ml bottle of chocolate milk, cheering his good fortune—he'd gotten £1.40 from people and ended up eating better than any of us.

It's the purest of bullshit speculation and armchair psychology, but I wondered, in hindsight, if Scott hadn't learned a dangerous lesson that day, about the good will of others, and the degree he could exploit it. I do know by the time I dropped out of the college scene myself, some of the tales of money owed by Scott to friends were scary.

And then there's the last time I saw him.

Eleven years ago. I was working and living in London, in University Admin. The campus was pretty well spread out and I was walking back from some briefing to the office with a couple of colleagues. It was summer and bright, and I had mirrored John Lennon shades, because... Because Scott used to wear them, he was the first kid in school that did, and all those years later, I still thought they were the coolest.

Jesus, things you don't realise until you start writing. I can see why people don't.

Anyhow, so this lovely summer day, I'm walking down the sunny London street, and after I cross the road and head towards my office, chatting with my co-worker, we walk past a homeless guy begging.

And it's Scott.

I freeze and just stare for a second. It's kind of a shock. He's put on weight and he looks dirty and down, but it's definitely him. And I say, 'Scott?'

His eyes narrow; he looks shifty and uncomfortable and sort of says, 'Yee...umm, who are you?' Or something like that.

And I flick my glasses to the end of my nose so he can see my eyes. 'It's Kit, man.'

The weariness, the shiftiness, just drops straight from his face, which is kind of lovely, and then he smiles a big, real smile, which is lovelier. 'Kit! Hey man! I didn't recognize you, until you did the...'

And he mimes flicking sunglasses down his nose. And I think, yeah, Scott, that was your move, you used to do it all the time with your Lennon shades, and I thought it was the coolest thing, so I copied you, and now you're smiling at me doing it because I guess you forgot all about how you used to do it or whatever. And fucking hell that felt strange, and sad.

We chatted a bit, mostly him rambling about his music ('we got the album done... and no one's bought it! We couldn't sell two copies if we pressed a double'—first time I ever heard that joke too, actually), his girl troubles ('...she just doesn't understand...') I bunged him a couple of quid and we made a lunch date (him: 'What do we want? Pub lunch! When do we want it? Umm [mimes looking at watch] about... 1 – 1:30ish?')

I went back to the office, and went back out at 1pm to buy him lunch, but he didn't show.

And that was the last time I saw him.

It fucked me up, too; I remember that. I went on about it to my dad, my co-workers—hell, my wife knows the story, knew it before my sister phoned with the news—OD of course, heroin, of course, funeral back in Devon, no fucking thank you. I remember that evening, in the pub that was the then-future-site of my magnificent Karaoke triumph, telling a co-worker about what had happened that day, telling Scott stories and how sad I was about where he'd ended up. And I remember her saying to me, 'But you know you were right to worship him, right? You know he's going to rise above.'

Scott, man, I wish she'd been right. I wish that so damn much.

RIP man. You were the coolest motherfucker in school. I'll miss you.

OLD MAN, WHY DO YOU SMOKE?

POSTSCRIPT: Or, What Have We Learned?

WARNING: What follows is political. Not party political, but political all the same. If the notion of talking about politics in the face of what you've just read offends you, I understand, and please stop reading now.

For the rest of you, I have some shit to talk about.

Because, sure, one of the things the above clearly demonstrates is just how much life can be like a shitty, badly-written novel, all coincidence and happenstance and patterns that only occur after it's too late for anything to be done. To tease out only the most obvious example from the above, the 'DC record he gave me is the first one after Bon Scott died. I mean to say, it's a record written in the shadow of the death of a singer killed by his addictions. That's an obscenity no decent novelist would dare invent. It's fucking pathetic. And none of that is invalid, but that's also not why I'm sitting here, listening to AC/DC's *Back in Black* album on vinyl with angry tears down my face, thinking about my smart, charismatic, lying, sweet, violent, unreliable, talented dead friend.

I'm sat here feeling shitty because he died. Because, complicated and frustrating and messed up as Scott was, the world was a better and more interesting place with him in it. Unquestionably. Not to belabour the point, but any kid who can be embarrassed at fourteen about the songs he wrote when he was 'younger' is a kid who has—had—something to offer. Something a tad more meaningful and important than a heroin overdose.

And, you know, a few people have tried to tell me it's a tragedy. Well, I've given it a lot of thought, and I've come to the considered opinion that it's nothing of the fucking kind. It's a travesty, not a tragedy.

Scott shouldn't have died. And he needn't have. His death, self-inflicted as it undoubtedly was, was also pathetically preventable.

Scott was a casualty in a war. The hands down dumbest war Western powers have ever engaged in. A war that is unwinnable, costs billions each year, and creates nothing but full prisons, suffering, and death.

Scott was yet another casualty in the war on drugs. And I am fucking livid about it.

Because here's what happened to Scott.

Scott had gotten clean. Gotten himself a girl. Was settled back home in Devon. Working? Hell if I know. But he'd got himself back on track.

And then, seemingly out of the blue, decided to go to London on a bender.

So far, so predictable-shitty-melodrama-plot-twist.

Here's the problem, though. This is the point where our nations stupid drug policy stepped in and stepped on Scott. Because he hadn't used in a good while, his levels of tolerance were far lower than he reasonably might have thought. Additionally, because he bought his heroin on the street—as opposed to, oh, I dunno, getting it from a pharmacist or doctor who could give him an appropriate dosage and purity and advised him of the risks of OD when returning to the substance after a period of absence— he had precisely zero clue how strong it was, or what else it was cut with.

OLD MAN, WHY DO YOU SMOKE?

And so he OD'd. And so he's dead.

And I can hear some of you piping up in indignant reply, giving it *personal responsibility*, giving it *he knew the risks*, maybe with a ragged chorus of *you can't save everyone*, and that most bathetic of middle eights about how *his death will serve as a lesson*. And to all of that, I say, with the greatest possible respect—fuck you. You don't know what you are talking about, and you need to fuck off and educate yourself.

Because as much as we still don't understand about addiction, there is one thing that the medical professionals are all agreed on, and if you found yourself mentally rehearsing any of the above arguments, this is a message you urgently need to hear, and the message is this: Addiction is an illness. Period.

Not a weakness of character. Not a corruption of moral values. Not laziness, or hedonism, not the devil, nor any of the other bullshit reasons you give yourself to harden your heart and dismiss those afflicted with this disease as unworthy of your compassion, or of society's help. Nope, all the medical professionals agree, overwhelmingly. Addiction is a disease.

And if you give it more than a second's thought, you'll realize the truth of it yourself. Because why the fuck else would people do it? Why would people go back and back and back again, to the bottle or the card table or the needle, with the sure and certain knowledge that they were risking their own destruction? Most of the people reading this like a drink now and then. Most of them also recognize that getting drunk every night (or every lunchtime) is a bad idea, and don't do it. Actually, scratch that—*everyone* reading this understands that's a bad idea. It's just that, statistically, some of you know that and do it anyway, because you can't stop. Because you have an illness, called addiction, and it overrides rationality.

It's a fucking illness. Only unlike every other illness, we don't treat this one with medicine and health professionals. We treat it with prison. With punishment. What we do, what we actually do, is take people suffering from a disease, and command them to be well, under pain of incarceration.

Oh, and also, we kill them. By denying them safe, measured and monitored access to the substances that they are going to find and use anyway, come hell or high water, we kill them. By taking Scott, and instead of saying to him, 'here's treatment for your addiction, but if you do fall off, come here and we'll make sure you get a dose that will scratch the itch without killing you,' we say, 'fuck you junkie scum, get your ass out on the street, and good luck.'

And I don't want to live in this fucking world. I don't.

Because here's the bottom line: if we treated cancer patients like this—blamed them for their condition, sent them out on the street to try back alley radiotherapy or chemo… ah, fuck it, I can't even be bothered to finish the metaphor, not because it's invalid, but because you've already grasped the absurdity, bordering on obscenity, that such an approach would represent.

Well, hold that thought. Because that's actually

the world you live in, right now. Unless you're lucky enough to live in Portugal, you live in a society where every day, sick members of your population are criminalized for the fact of their disease. Are denied treatment for their addictions. And, consequently, are killed, by ignorance and fear.

There's a whole tangent here about mental health, and our pathetic inability to identify mental health issues as 'real'—or at least, as real as physical health issues—but it's late, and I'm tired, drunk and depressed enough. For now, just hold the image of the cancer patients in your mind, and understand that it's no fucking different for the addict.

No. Fucking. Different.

My friend wasn't really my friend. I know that. I also know I loved him, and I was right to love him. And I know he's dead, and he shouldn't be.

I may not be able to do anything practical about that fact. But I will, forever and always, be angry, furious, at the idiotic laws and processes and people that allowed my friend to die, when he could—and should—have lived.

Because what Scott has taught me is this: *never* blame the victim.

Never.

NOW IT'S TIME TO SHOW YOU WHAT I ALREADY KNOW

The Thing

Tough to be sure, but I'm going to go ahead and blame this one on Uncle Edward. He had a pretty sizable VHS collection of movies recorded off the telly. They sat behind glass in a cabinet, row after row of identical plastic cases with faux hardback book colouration and gold leaf edging, differentiated only by numbers stuck to the spines. To decode what was going on, you needed The Book—an A5 notebook with a number per page, corresponding to the number on the cases and tapes. The book served a dual function—it was the listing, so you knew what was on each tape, but it was also a kind of cultural archaeological catalogue. For example, a typical entry might read:

15A:
When Harry Met Sally—WATCHED!
Carebears the movie 2—WATCHED!
Police Academy 3—WATCHED!
Eastenders Christmas special—WATCHED!
Mr. Jolly Lives Next Door—WATCHED!
Ghostbusters—KEEP!

See? I really think, looking back, you could have

learned almost everything you needed to know about the cultural taste of the person whose house you were sitting in if you could just get five or ten minutes with The Book.

Anyway.

Uncle Edward had a similarly relaxed approach to the notion of video certification as the Video Van Man. My uncle's policy was, if you could read the name of the film you wanted to watch, you could watch it. To be perfectly fair, he'd sit and watch it with you. So, you know, responsibly irresponsible.

(Total aside, he also had what was to me a bizarre and borderline sacrilegious habit of turning the film off the second it ended, which was diametrically opposed to my father's mute insistence on watching the entire credit crawl before leaving the theatre/turning the lights on and getting up. I mean, what a weirdo, right?)

I wish I could tell you how old I was. Too young, is all I can reasonably say.

'Uncle Edward, what's *The Thing*?'

'Oh, that's the one about the alien at the North Pole that kills people. It's good. Want to stick it on?'

Oh, my, yes.

This film, man. The music, for starters—this minimalist single bass pulse, broadcasting menace. The opening, a helicopter chasing a husky, shooting at it, drunk Kirk Russell pouring scotch into his computer because it's beaten him at chess, the head of the base shooting the pilot through the eye (as an extremely gruesome close up of the body confirms)—we're five minutes in, and already I've all but overdosed on awesome.

I know people bang on about the central premise, and it's not to be ignored—a great example of simplicity being genius. Arctic base, huge storm, small group of people, and one or more of them is actually an alien lifeform that can consume and then duplicate any other lifeform. I mean, come *on,* people. But I have to say, that's not my abiding memory of the film. No, the thing that sticks with me the most, the moments seared into my memory, are the goddamn creature effects.

Because they are insane. I mean, off the hook batshit crazy. Example: The husky from earlier is put into a cage with the other huskies. The men become aware that something may be wrong with it—it may not be what it seems. They head down to the holding pen. It's badly lit. They can hear whining, the other dogs in distress. While they fuck about trying to find a light, we get to see the dogs. They appear to have been skinned and impaled on tentacles. There's a moment when the suspect husky is growling, snarling, and then its snout splits open four ways, revealing teeth, raw red flesh, and a tongue that whips and grows, becoming one of those deadly tentacles. It happens with a loud snapping noise, is my memory, and I just about leapt out of my skin.

I stayed there for the duration, paralysed with awe at the enormity of it—this creature could do anything, transmute its flesh at will. I saw a mouth open in the chest of an apparently dead man, with huge teeth that proceeded to amputate the hands of the doctor applying the paddles. I then watched in mute numb shock as that body was burned, and the head of the body stretched its neck until the tissue

NOW IT'S TIME TO SHOW YOU...

became thin enough for the head to tear free, whereupon it fell to the floor, sprouted eight legs, and scuttled away.

When the dazed tech, seeing this, utters flatly, 'You gotta be fucking kidding me,' I don't think I've ever concurred more with a verbally expressed sentiment.

The other big set-piece I vividly remember is when the remaining survivors are rounded up and tied to chairs as Russell explains his theory that every cell of the creature is alive and will independently attempt to survive. He then draws blood from each survivor, and places the samples in labelled Petri dishes, one per man. He proceeds to heat up a copper wire, and go through each blood sample in turn.

The tension is unbelievable. I can still picture the scene with near total recall, what, twenty years back? Has to be. This is cinema. This is what movies are supposed to deliver—something that burns itself into your brain and will not let go. Introduce an idea—it can look like anything or anyone living, and has effectively fluid flesh—and then just run it pedal to the metal. I know a lot of people my age were enamoured of and freaked out by the T1000 and the liquid metal idea, but I have to tell you, it had nothing on this flesh and bone monstrosity.

This was horror. It was like a *Doctor Who* story turned up to 99 with no Doctor to save everyone. It scared the living shit out of me.

I fucking loved it.

And now I'm going to go watch it with my fifteen-year-old stepdaughter who's never seen it before.

Back soon.

***

Well, okay, yeah. It's pretty much as good as I remember.

I mean, you wouldn't pace a movie that slowly anymore. You just would not. You wouldn't, for example, fly out to the other base twice—no way. You'd contrive a reading of the map while you were there the first time, to get the exposition solved in one hit. I also don't think you'd use fadeouts that imply the uneventful passage of days. It's a little dismaying how much pacing has tightened in cinema in the last—fucking hell, the last thirty years. Fuck, I'm old.

Enough of that bullshit—basically, yes, it *is* still awesome. There's essentially two superb movies going on—one a tense psychological paranoid drama, fantastically played with real understated intelligence by the cast. In particular, I'd forgotten how great the autopsies are—there's a fantastic moment where Blair bends to start cutting up the lumpen dog creature, and the look in his eyes, the set of his jaw—man, I just cackled.

And then there are those creatures. Oh my sweet lord. The dog lump carcass and the twisted burnt man-thing they bring back from the other base are incredible, dark creations. The way the latter steams as Blair pulls out the internal organs, carefully cataloguing, displays a disturbing attention to detail. The aforementioned head spider sequence deserved every bit of WTF love I gave it as a kid, and I'd forgotten the moment immediately after the blood test goes south (oh yeah, hearing my stepdaughter scream when the petri dish exploded was a particular highlight) and Palmer, the one you'd been carefully led to not suspect, Things out in spectacular fashion, to the extent that his whole head splits in half down to his neck, revealing rows of sharp teeth, which he then proceeds to use to eat the head of one of the other survivors. In the meantime, Kurt Russell wins the Grand Prize for Failure To Remember How To Operate A Flamethrower At The Most Inopportune Possible Fucking Moment.

Okay, that sounds utterly insane and gross, and it is, but it's also a kind of genius: I maintain it takes incredible imagination to come up with this stuff, and the skill in the execution is breathtaking—as my Dad observed afterwards, 'Digital's cool, but you can't beat mechanics, can you?' You really, *really* can't, and the reason is simple once you think about it: the mechanics are real. The Thing is actually in the room with the actors, interacting with them. And the most advanced physics simulator and texture mappers in the world still can't quite pull that off. And, I know, 'give it five years Granddad,' and you're right—but as of today, the point stands.

So does *The Thing*. Everything about those monster action sequences is exquisite—the editing, the sound, the coverage, the creature effects, the acting. They must have been nightmares to shoot, they must have cost a fortune and taken weeks, and all for just minutes of cinema that will absolutely blow your fucking head off. Sure, the pacing at the end is a little shonky, and I'm still unsure I follow the logic of 'let's just blow the whole base up' in the final fifteen minutes, but frankly it couldn't matter less. What matters is that in 1982, John Carpenter and the cast and crew of this film beat their brains bloody, pouring the best of their creativity and skill at moviemaking into crafting a piece of cinema that at a distance of thirty years can still shock, amaze, scare, and exult.

You gotta be fucking kidding me, indeed.

A TANKED UP MOB

Hillsborough

I was ten when Hillsborough happened. Unlike some earlier and later tragedies, I don't have a vivid memory of the event itself. As previously mentioned, my family didn't turn the news off, so I'd have seen it reported, but I have no immediate recollection of it. What I do have is an association of dread with the name. The very word casts a shadow inside. That kid's feeling of Something Bad. I knew Hillsborough was Something Bad. I knew that People Died. Were, in point of fact, crushed. The figure ninety-six hadn't registered. Nor had the whys and wherefores.

I didn't grow up in a football house. I'd nominally adopted Liverpool as my football team a few years before—the first televised football match I saw was Liverpool vs Barnsley, where Liverpool won two nil, good enough for me—but truthfully I said that just so I had an answer to the question 'who do you support?' I never voluntarily watched a match on TV, or even highlights after the news.

Hillsborough bled into the background horror of the news in the 80s—African famine, the miners' strike, Challenger. Hillsborough. Another word indicating something dreadful, a horror that dropped out of a clear blue sky to kill people at a football match.

I didn't have a personal connection. I didn't lose anyone, nor did anyone in my family. I was aware of the campaign for justice, but never engaged with it beyond a 'wow, *The Sun* have really *always* been Scum, haven't they?' kind of way. And, you know, I've read a lot of the recent coverage, and I'm unsure I have a single original observation—I'm not convinced that anything I'm about to write hasn't been said better, more clearly, by someone with a more personal stake than me. But it's gone 1am on a Friday night at the end of a long week, and instead of sleeping, I'm not sleeping, because this fucking story is rattling around in my head.

So here we are.

It's the verdict, of course. Twenty-seven years later, the crime has finally been admitted. Except that's not quite right, is it? More accurately, in a majority verdict, a coroner's jury has confirmed that ninety-six Liverpool supporters were unlawfully killed, and bore no culpability for their own demise.

And really, there's no point in me trying to rehash it. I'm just going to assume you know what happened, how it was denied, and the recent court result. If you don't, and you have twenty minutes, Google: 'Hillsborough Disaster Deadly Mistakes And Lies That Lasted Decades'. Be warned—it's heavy stuff.

No, what I've been trying to figure out is why this one has me so upset. Such a curious mixture of vindication, validation, and anger. Because, again, fundamentally, it's not my fucking fight. Not even close. So why this potent, nauseating cocktail that has me obsessively reading, tweeting, sharing, and finally writing about an event that occurred in my childhood, and about which, truthfully, I basically haven't engaged with in any depth until this week?

A TANKED UP MOB

And by the way, I actively avoided opportunities to educate myself. That's worth noting. Jimmy McGovern, the man who wrote the greatest TV show of the 90s (*Cracker*) wrote a docudrama in 1997 called *Hillsborough*. Starring Christopher Eccleston, for fucks sake. And I ducked it. Didn't want it. Couldn't. Too scared. How is that possible? How was I too scared of a story I didn't know? What is that, exactly?

Anyway.

This week, suddenly, I couldn't get enough. And in trying to make sense of why, okay, let's start here: I think it was Watergate that first spawned the saying, 'It's not the scandal that gets you, it's the cover up.' And what is now crystal clear, a matter of historical record, is that there *was* a cover up. This is not paranoid lefty bollocks. This is fact (The Truth, if you will). South Yorkshire Police engaged in a conspiracy to cover up negligence that led to the deaths of ninety-six people. This happened.

And the first thing to say is, yes, the police on the ground on the day fucked up. The man in charge didn't have the first clue what he was doing, having been transferred into the job two weeks prior (not his fault) and did absolutely nothing to acquaint himself with the grounds or the known issues with crowd control surrounding said grounds (absolutely his fault). It's worth remembering that the verdict also confirms that the design of the stadium was at fault too, as was the city council that approved this public space for use. In other words, this was a disaster waiting to happen. It should not have been possible for a fuck up in crowd control by the police to lead to a lethal incident. And indeed, nowadays, it isn't. Lessons about football stadium design were learned. It really couldn't happen again today.

Nonetheless, it hadn't happened before at this ground (though there had been a couple of close calls in recent memory, at the '81 and '88 semi-final matches, and there had been previous stadium disasters overseas—most infamously at Heysel, Brussels, in 1985, an incident that also involved Liverpool fans and a lethal crush. I'll come back to Heysel, alas—it's vital to the context). And the reason it had not gotten lethal before at Hillsborough was that the officer in charge knew that the access to the pen area was dangerous, and put careful countermeasures in place to prevent disaster. In short, he did his fucking job.

On 15th April, 1989, the officer in charge spectacularly failed in that same job. He made literally fatal errors.

So far, so understandable—so inevitable, even, perhaps. Shitty stadium design plus dodgy health and safety certificate plus inexperienced officer in charge equals awful, dreadful tragedy. It could have ended there. It should have ended there. Lessons learned, an end to that kind of stadium design, no more standing pens, and yeah, maybe an officer or two loses their job for incompetence. A city and nation mourns, and then we learn the lessons and life goes on.

It should have ended there.

Instead, we had the cover up.

It started—and this is not a gaudy turn of phrase, but a matter of historical record—before the bodies were even cold.

A TANKED UP MOB

Can you even conceive of it? Try this on: at 3:15pm, fifteen minutes after the match was supposed to have kicked off, with the bodies of the dead and dying still being pulled from the stands onto the pitch, while rank and file officers and swamped paramedics and members of the public ripped up advertising hoarding to make stretchers and frantically attempted CPR, the officer in charge was telling the secretary of the Football Association that drunken ticketless Liverpool fans had forced open an exit gate and stormed the grounds, leading to the lethal crush. The only slight flaw with this story being that the fans all held valid tickets, and the officer himself had given the order to open the gate twenty-three minutes before.

Men, women and children were still dying, in circumstances and under conditions that are the equal of any horror the most callous author could dare conceive, and this officer was already putting in place the scaffolding for the Big Lie—a lie that would, in various mutated forms, haunt the victims' families for twenty-seven years.

That lie didn't last the day. Footage of enraged and distraught survivors waving intact tickets put paid to it. But in the meantime, with modification, the cover up gained pace. And The Big Lie morphed into its most infamous form—a form, incidentally, that is these days recognized as a ubiquitous and pernicious problem when it comes to criminal activity that people seek to excuse. I speak, of course, of victim blaming.

Here's what happened next: to bolster the already crumbling story of the ticketless fans and the forced gate, the spin became that the fans were drunk. To try and verify this, officers were dispatched—and again, this happened literally before the bodies were cold—to photograph the litter bins and detritus that accumulated outside and in the pens, to look for empty alcohol containers (of which, as surviving photos show, there were precious few). And how about this? The bodies of the victims were all taken to a nearby gymnasium, where blood samples were taken from the corpses to ascertain the level of alcohol consumption of the victims. One of the sampled corpses was that of a ten-year-old boy. The bodies remained in the gym. Photographs were taken of the victims, and piles of these Polaroids were given to relatives, to sort through and identify missing loved ones. Officers then immediately questioned these grieving relatives about the alcohol consumption of the deceased.

This happened.

There was a reason for all this. It wasn't random malice. It was an attempt to construct a counter narrative to the truth. It was a flagrant and calculated effort to cover up police incompetence that led to ninety-six deaths.

This really happened. In my lifetime, this really happened.

And this was all the set up for what would happen that evening. That evening, the local Conservative MP met with police officers involved in the afternoon's events. He was told by several officers that the fans were 'pissed out of their minds,' that supporters had 'pissed on' and punched police during the rescue operations. That 'it was booze what done it,' that drunken louts had caused and exacerbated the tragedy. Oh, and that survivors had looted the bodies of the dead.

Yeah, you read that right.

We know the last claim is categorically false. We know, because the police meticulously inventoried the possessions of the deceased, as they must. That is to say, they knew this was a lie when they were telling it.

Not crass enough? Missing that perfect hypocritical, too-gross-to-be-invented kicker? Here it comes: This briefing took place in a police bar, where officers were drinking to forget the terrible things they'd witnessed that day. The people telling lies about 'drunken louts' causing a disaster were not only telling lies in an organised conspiracy to blame the victims and cover up the real perpetrators in the force, but they were likely drunk themselves while they did it.

A Tanked Up Mob, indeed.

This same briefing was given to government ministers and the Prime Minister the following day. And, of course, the press. This led *The Sun* to print a front-page splash even more notorious in British publishing history than *The Mail*'s Nazi-loving 'Hurrah for the Blackshirts'—listing the above fabrications as facts under the headline The Truth.

Does it still count as irony if it makes you want to burn things down?

Anyway.

To cut an (incredibly) long story (obscenely) short, the lie stuck for twenty-seven years, and then a coroner's jury ruled that the deaths were a result of criminal negligence, the end. Except that's bollocks, it's not the end, and not just because there will almost certainly be criminal trials, after which some of the senior officers involved may well go to jail, and also maybe civil cases, but for at least two other reasons—the reasons for which I'm up so very far past my bedtime, hammering at this poor keyboard.

Number one: This cover up happened. South Yorkshire police conspired to cover up negligence that resulted in ninety-six deaths. That's a fact. That's now a matter of historical record, not leftie paranoia, or anti-Tory, *Sun* or establishment propaganda. The verdict is unambiguous: the victims were not to blame.

Hold that thought. Now consider again—the cover up started rolling before the bodies were cold.

What does that suggest, to you? Because I'll tell you what it suggests to me. It suggests, rather strongly, that we're dealing with an institution with not just an instinct to cover up, but also an instinctive understanding of *how* to cover up. The response to this disaster was quick, and decisive, and coordinated. Before the last person had been declared dead at the scene (let alone posthumously tested for blood alcohol levels), officers were putting in place the lie that, with modification, they would cling to for nearly three decades. That required coordination. That required officers at several layers of command to play ball—enough to, in turn, intimidate the rank and file sufficiently to ensure that the conspiracy of silence that all cover ups require to function would hold.

You know what that tells me?

A TANKED UP MOB

This was not South Yorkshire police's first rodeo. It almost cannot have been.

And oh brothers and sisters, that scares the shit out of me.

Because it's one thing to suspect it; one thing to say, in a dry and intellectual way, 'well of course it was a different era, and I'm sure corners got cut and whatnot,' but it's quite a different proposition to learn that, when you were growing up, a police force that was, now I think of it, my local cops, were geared up to provide institutional cover-ups on incredibly short notice, should the body count require it. If that doesn't disturb you, I do not understand you as a human being. I may envy you, but I don't understand you at all.

And that leads us neatly to point number two: how in the hell did this stick? How can it possibly have taken twenty-seven years to prove that such an obvious fabrication was a lie?

And here's where I have to drop into a brief digression concerning 80s era football hooliganism and the attendant tabloid moral panic. I will keep it brief.

UK football fans had a dreadful reputation in the 80s, mainly due to incidences of fan violence between rival club supporters. These cases were especially bad during international competitions, and at the worst such incident, in 1985 at Heysel stadium, Brussels, thirty-nine fans were killed and six hundred injured. The deaths occurred when the English supporters charged a group of Italian fans across the stands. The Italian fans fled to a concrete wall, where the lethal crush occurred. The wall collapsed, and afterwards many tried to blame the deaths on that collapse. However, subsequent evidence has shown that the deaths occurred before the collapse of the wall, and indeed it's likely that the collapse saved lives.

In due course, twenty-six English supporters would stand trial for manslaughter in relation to their actions that day, and fourteen would be convicted. The stadium management and governing bodies that oversaw the match would in due course also receive censure for their failures in assuring safety, which contributed to the disaster.

The impact on British football was tremendous. There was a blanket ban of five years on all English clubs, with a higher penalty for the club whose supporters had been directly involved. The British Prime Minister, Margaret Thatcher, declared that 'those responsible had brought shame and disgrace to their country.'

Margaret Thatcher was still prime minister when the Hillsborough disaster occurred.

And the English club that were playing Juventus on 29th May 1985 was, of course, Liverpool FC.

Do you see now? Do you understand how easy it was to stick The Lie? Because, of course, it's Scouse football fans. What can you expect?

The Lie stuck because of gross stereotypes about football fans, Liverpudlians, and wider stereotypes about the working class and alcoholism. It stuck because there was *just enough* smoke, and the people in power were craven enough to exploit it to cover up their failings.

That smoke has a name, and the name is prejudice.

A TANKED UP MOB

And when deployed in this way, it serves only to obscure truth.

And again, if that casual utilization of prejudice to protect the powerful at the expense of the innocent doesn't chill you to the bone, I'm not saying we can't be friends, but I don't understand you.

Because what happened was that lazy stereotypes about a particular class of people were effectively weaponised to a) implicate and criminalize blameless victims, and render them complicit in their own deaths and b) protect a criminally negligent establishment from the consequences of its faults.

The 80s was a different era. One of the many ways it was different from now is how much higher the tolerance was for humour and dialogue in general based on stereotypes. And, you know, there are still people who bemoan the end of that era. 'Why doesn't anyone have a sense of humour any more?' 'Why can't I call people an <offensive slur> any more? It's just a joke!' Above all, that. *It's just a joke*. Like those jokes about Scousers: hubcap thieves, alcoholics, hooligans. Pushy. Ignorant. Bad hair, bad teeth, bad manners. Promiscuous. Not too bright. Kind of stupid actually.

Stupid violent thieving drunkards.

Get it yet? Do you?

Because this is how it happens. *Exactly* how it happens. You start with 'harmless jokes,' stereotypes, and to use a currently fashionable phrase, microaggressions. And it's harmless, right? *Wassamatter, can't take a joke? Got no sense of humour?*

But it sticks. It festers. It lingers. In the wider

psyche, in the general population. Because here's The Truth, people—*The Sun* ran that headline, and it didn't go out of business. Outside of Merseyside (where to this day the paper is not read, and the name itself so offensive as to be censored by local press as *The S*n*, a fact that is to the eternal credit of the people and journalists of Liverpool) 'The Truth' was widely read, absorbed, and believed. Why? How? Because this vicious, disgusting lie fitted a convenient pre-existing stereotype. I'm not one for the slippery slope argument, as a rule—truth to tell, I think it's most often used as a way of resisting essential change by extrapolating to some ridiculous extreme, but it's hard to deny a proof as visceral and clear. Indeed, it would be obtuse. This is where 'harmless' stereotyping leads—to convenient scapegoats when those in authority who have fucked up royally want to find someone to blame. I know, I know, reads like leftie bullshit. Well, fuck you bucko—it fucking happened. For real, in my country, in my lifetime, it fucking happened.

In my lifetime, a police force covered up what is now, as a matter of historical record, negligence that led to the unlawful deaths of ninety-six blameless citizens. And at least a part of how the lie stuck so firm for so long was this disgusting stereotype. 'Oh well, you know, Scousers. No sense of humor. Can't let things go. Grievance culture. Still banging on about Hillsborough. Still don't buy *The Sun*. Hey, did you hear the one about when I parked my car in Liverpool?'

Tanked Up Yobs. That's how Bernard Ingham described the dead victims of police negligence. That was the stereotype the families of the victims have fought against for twenty-seven years, in the face of a hostile establishment and an apathetic public, extending to people like me who effectively said 'wow, that sounds sad/depressing' and changed the channel before I could be bummed out.

And I mean, to those survivors, and to those families of survivors, some fucking writer I am, because I have no words. I can't comprehend the pain you have faced, have lived with, every day for twenty-seven years. I cannot begin to imagine—or maybe I just don't want to—your incredulity, your outrage, at each setback, each official denial and lie, each miscarriage of justice. I literally cannot conceive of what you have been through, and all I can do is salute your courage, your stubbornness, your indefatigability, in pursuing the cause of justice for the ones you lost.

I guess I can also say thank you. Thank you for not giving up. Thank you for not giving in. Thank you for chasing this one all the way, for never letting the forces arrayed against you prevent you from seeking justice for your loved ones. You have not just honoured their memory. You have not merely rescued their reputation from lies and deceit. You have cast light into darkness, exposed injustice, and set history straight. For that, I am and remain grateful and humbled. You have rendered us all an incredible service. Not so much 'professional victims' as tireless campaigners for truth and justice. Thank you. Thank you. Thank you.

To everyone else; the next time that boring leftie friend gives you shit for some intemperate comment about some minority or religious or disabled group—any sentence you might think about uttering that includes the word 'they' or 'them', basically—and you find yourself about to reply, verbally or perhaps only internally, 'WTF dude? Don't you have a sense of humour?' please, please, think about this. Think about how thousands, millions of tiny jokes and off-hand comments, built, slowly but surely, a monument, a calcified statue that encased and marginalized and finally dehumanized real people, actual humans, people like you and me who just wanted to go and watch a football match. Then think about how, by cynically exploiting that stereotype, people in power and authority covered up negligence that led to the deaths of ninety-six ordinary citizens—men, women, children. A cover up that lasted twenty-seven years.

Yeah, it couldn't have happened without a corrupt police force. True.

It also couldn't have happened without the stereotype.

Which of those two factors do you, personally, exert some control over?

Now, ask yourself if you'd want to have to wait—worse, not wait, fight, fight with everything you have, all your energy, money, focus, dedicated to this struggle—for twenty-seven years, for justice for your wife. Your brother.

Your child.

You would. I know you would. So would I.

But wouldn't you rather not need to?

#JusticeForThe96

THIS MONSTER THAT WE CALL THE EARTH IS BLEEDING

The Headless Children

It starts with blackness. How could it not? Hovering in the darkness, a skull. Its huge jaw unhinged in an endless scream; flames and smoke curl up behind it, and streaming from the mouth of the skull, an army of the damned. Klansmen. Hitler. Ruby, shooting Oswald. Dictators. Tyrants. Despots. Killers.

It's 1989. I am still eleven.

A choir, discordant, then a single picking guitar, minor chords. Then a second. Bass drum now, beating a tattoo. The guitars swirl, one low, one high, building, and then a sudden drum roll…

And we're off.

The pace is a gallop, guitars chugging with that BC Rich snarl, like chainsaws. Vocals growling, high. Spinning tales of lost souls, brother murdering brother, drowning in blood, the cycle of violence become a spiral.

Welcome to 'Heretic (the lost child)', opening track of the magnum opus of LA cock-turned-shock rockers (fans of *The Crimson Idol*—you're wrong, and shut up) W.A.S.P.—*The Headless Children*.

W.A.S.P. are a metal band from LA. The bastard child of KISS, Iron Maiden and Alice Cooper, their primary strength is the lead singer/songwriter Blackie Lawless—a six foot snarling long-haired freak with an incredible rock voice and distinctive style, heavy on the powerful, fast paced riffage. For three albums, they had written songs about getting laid, mainly, and built a decent following on the back of live performances featuring homemade smoke machines, circular saw blade codpieces, and Blackie pretending to drink pig's blood from a human skull at the climax of any given show.

If that sounds like good clean dirty dumb fun, I'm telling it about right. For all the snarl, W.A.S.P. are as threatening as a horny poodle. But following the live album release, something happens for Blackie. Something changes. And when he heads back to the studio, his head is buzzing with ideas that have nothing to do with his libido and everything to do with the state of the world. That always colossal riff machine is about to get hooked to an altogether darker, more powerful engine…

There's an urgency to the playing, a frantic energy, but it's coupled with solid skills—they've been together for eight years now and they're tight. The riffs are deceptive—they are basic, but there's these little flourishes that show real flair. For the first time, Blackie's trademark vocal attack sounds haunted, desperate. When the outro begins he sings:

Don't turn out the lights
'cause there's demons in the night
and they prey on the fears of us all…

It sounds like he means it. It's the soundtrack to a

horror apocalypse—zombie, plague, nuclear annihilation, pick your poison. It's an anthem for the end of the world, not a celebration but a funeral dirge, played at 80 BPM, raging against the dying of the light. The outro rolls on and on, relentless, building and building, furiously played.

That's song one.

Then it's 'The Real Me'. Tough one, this. I mean, listened to in isolation, without context, it's awesome—the lyric textbook alienated youth, a killer bass line twinned with a brilliant broken guitar riff. The middle eight with just vox, bass and drums is particularly fine, and Blackie's voice is on fire throughout. When you're eleven, it's near perfect. But then you grow up, you discover The Who wrote it twenty odd years before W.A.S.P. recorded it, and that… takes the shine off a bit. But it's one hell of a performance, and they make it sound like a W.A.S.P. song, and as someone who as an adult has covered a few songs, I can tell you that's no mean feat.

Anyway, enough of that. The choir has started, and the main event is about to begin.

'The Headless Children' is an immense track. The intro guitars play a slower, menacing riff as all the sounds of a horror movie swirl in your headphones, demonic laughter, howling feedback, and indistinguishable animal sounds, before it fades to a hammer horror keyboard reverb—and then the chorus riff, no vocal, just giving us a taste…

Father come save us from this madness we're under
God of creation are you blind?

MY LIFE IN HORROR VOLUME I

This is the moment. This song. This is the point where my young brain grasped that horror didn't always have to be something you were scared of. It could be something you owned. That you created. That you could take all the darkest parts of your terrified imagination and vomit them back out in some powerful, creative act. That not only was it okay to be scared, it was mandatory, because the world was a scary, dark place, and to ignore or diminish that was to deny reality, take the path of cowardice. No, the only true path, the only valid response, was to stare into the darkness, catalogue it as best you could, wrestle with it, understand what you could of it. And by so doing, render some kind of dark celebration. It was the understanding that fury in response to the world was valid, even necessary, a precondition to meaningful self-expression.

And look, cards on the table, can this song, on this album, really bare the weight of all that? Isn't it just a question of time plus place plus brain chemistry times the first stirrings of puberty minus a sense of perspective? Well, yes, sure. And no, not at all. I mean, all of these essays carry some of that, right? I was a child/teenager/young 'adult', and my brain was wired fundamentally differently. However, I've been listening to the album while writing this, and this track… still has it, kids. Yeah, the choir synth at the start carbon dates it, but the lyrics, vocal style and riffs, while clearly a product of time and place, nonetheless don't sound quite like anything I've heard before or since, and that counts for something.

More though, much more importantly, it still

speaks to my gut, still bypasses my brain and heads down direct to my neck muscles, and sets off the nod.

Next up is 'Thunderhead', which is probably the most unintentionally hilarious song about drug addiction ever written. Back to back with 'The Headless Children', jarring doesn't even cut it—it's like watching *Return of the Living Dead* after *Night of the Living Dead,* only if they'd been made by the same person who wanted you to take them both seriously. The piano and choir combo suddenly sounds pretentious, especially when the strings start in, and it's not helped by the fact that the (admittedly pretty damn fine) riff that clicks in has little if anything to do musically with what's proceeded. And yes, it's a great riff, and the drumming is immense, but the 'Hey! Hey! Hey!' in the chorus just about finishes it off. We've gone from horror movie soundtrack so good you don't need the actual movie to Spinal Tap does *Just Say No*.

This is where the bridge to the past breaks. I know I loved this as a kid, but I can't get back there now.

'Killer! You scream and you bleed! Thriller! You spread your disease!' screams Blackie as we head to the solo, and yeah, no, I'm no kind of expert wordsmith, but I'm pretty sure on alien planets there's creatures with eleven eyes and one ear picking that up on subspace radio and wincing before skipping the track.

Still, it's worth noting the horror movie motif continues as 'Thunderhead' communicates directly with the Demon H. It's a bad horror movie, but recognisably genre.

'Thunderhead, will you die for me?' 'Yes, Master!'

Bwahahahahahaha…

The solo is too long, and not terribly well played, though the reconnect to the chorus riff is deftly handled.

And that's it for side A. Just four tracks. That felt massive to me as well, as a kid. The idea that metal songs could be big and ambitious, with heft and scope. That music could be a journey. I may no longer be able to love 'Thunderhead', but to this day I am a sucker for a good ten-minute epic. I suspect you could trace the DNA of that particular taste back to this album.

(*Actually, we'll trace it further back, come* Volume II. *For now, though, let's say that while this observation is slightly misplaced in the general, where it still carries weight is insofar as this is probably the first time I felt this way about music I considered 'mine'; that is to say, not my parents. At eleven, that was already incredibly important to me.*)

Side B is never as good. It's a damn near immutable rule of rock, and not one that W.A.S.P. can subvert. We open with *Mean Man*, the nearest this album comes to a 'traditional' W.A.S.P. song. Chorus:

> *Cause I'm a mean/ motherfucking man*
> *I gotta Scream*
> *'Cause that's what I am*
> *All the w—a—a—y*
> *A- All the w—a—a—y!*

Written about guitarist Chris 'the brain cell' Holmes, it's about what you'd expect, complete with a borderline atrocious guitar solo, but a perfectly serviceable verse/chorus riff.

Far better is to follow, with *The Neutron Bomber*, Blackie's paranoid condemnation of 'Neutron Ronnie' (then-president Ronald Regan) as the harbinger of the apocalypse. And sure, it's easy to laugh now, in cosy old 2014, with the benefit of knowing the wall came down and the good guys won,[2] but it's worth stressing that in 1987, mutually assured destruction seemed as likely an outcome as any. Also, it's a killer track: the gallop is back, or at least a canter, and from the staccato concussive opening, we're into a great open chord building riff. Recasting Regan as a deranged pyromaniac is inspired.

Oh, 'till he dies he'll be burning inside

This too samples police sirens mixed with controlled feedback, and again, the feeling that you're hearing a soundtrack to a movie that never got released is damn near inescapable. It's a genuinely useful artefact for anyone who wants to try and make a case for historical inevitability (as in, listen to this and shut up) and, like Alan Moore's *Watchmen*, succeeds in making you feel fear, even as you know this particular world-ending threat is now no more than a ghost of a ghost. Captivating, and although my heart belongs to the title track, objectively (heh) there's every chance this is actually the best number on the album, if not the best song W.A.S.P. ever wrote.

---

[2] *For a given value of 'good guys' and 'won'.*

From there is the obligatory 'minor scale acoustic guitar instrumental to prove we can actually play' (it's an 80s thing) and then it's time for the single (which made the top 20 in the UK, because I saw the video on Top Of The Pops)—'Forever Free'.

And look, okay, Blackie's voice is incredible, but dear lord it's a veritable smorgasbord of hack rock cliché, from theme to lyric to tune to production to… *gah*, everything. Biker first person lead? Check. Girlfriend who probably should have obeyed the helmet laws? Check. Overdubbed repeat lyrics at the end of phrases that go, 'oh, no mooooore, no-owohwoah'? Check. Middle sixteen into minor key for guitar solo? Oh yes. Back out into repeated chorus, which drops to 'ooooooooooo' sung as a harmony as the guitar loops through the same pattern and the toms roll for a million years per end of phrase? Take an astute guess. Fade out finish? Please let's.

'Maneater' is far better fare, albeit hard to listen to post Rob Halford's coming out without a bit of a shameful snigger at the double entendre. This is where remembering being eleven helps a ton, because shorn of that association, the phrase gets to be as intended, chilling, horrific. And it's another classic pounding W.A.S.P. riff, with a particularly fine set of stabs before a cold stop into the chorus. While this re-listen has confirmed a lot of my worst suspicions about the quality of Mr Holmes guitar solos, I had forgotten what a monstrous riff machine W.A.S.P. could be in their prime, just how skilled they were at belting out heavier-than-hell-but-still-melodic tunes. And there's no way as a kid I could

THIS MONSTER THAT WE CALL THE EARTH...

possibly have appreciated what a rare talent Blackie has as a rock vocalist—the fact that he's not named in the same breath as obvious all-time greats Brian Johnson or Eddie Vedder (yeah, I went there) is a genuine travesty. It may not be to your taste, but it's a towering performance. Shove your juvenile homoerotic snark in the closet for a song (DYSWIDT?) and try and hear this one as intended—it rewards the effort.

We close out with 'Rebel In The F.D.G.' (Fucking Decadent Generation, so that's saved you a trip to Wikipedia—don't thank me, just keep buying my books). And there are two separate things to talk about here. The easy part is the song itself. Blackie's screamed opening line is superb, and it's a great little dirty walk-down riff, just a shade too heavy for *Dr. Feelgood* era Crüe. Some of the guitar breaks are short enough that even Chris Holmes can't fuck them up. Okay, the post guitar solo spoken section practically carbon dates another song, especially twinned with the hugely overproduced bass drum echo, but I'm not sure being a product of your times can be considered a hanging offence. It's also amusing that the final line of that section gets swallowed by rising guitars, eager to get back to the business of bashing out that chorus.

The second thing to note, and to my mind the more interesting, is the total incoherence of the lyric. As I've noted, W.A.S.P. were one of the exemplars of the cock rock scene, essentially boiling down Kiss and Alice Cooper to the dumbest component parts lyrically and the heaviest inclinations musically. Which, yes, that's a niche you can carve, and who am

I to etc. But there's something, oh, let's be insanely generous and say incongruous, about the band whose lead off EP was the one hundred per cent non-ironically titled *Fuck like a Beast* (yes, you read right) claiming to be in rebellion against the decadence of their own generation. As Bart Simpson might say, 'Wha'fuck, man?' (well, he might if I wrote him). Sure, Blackie is on record at the time as being (aside from alcohol) drug free, and I'm sure in the Hollywood rock scene of '87 that was at the very least eccentric, but if you're indulging in systematic sexual debauchery as part of a subculture with a well earned reputation for excess in this arena, claiming rebellion seems confused at best and self delusional at worst. Given what Blackie did next (and let's be honest, based on some of the more out-there moments on this, by far his most coherent and intelligent record) I know where I'd place my chips.

Regardless and very much in spite of that, 'The Headless Children' definitely represents an underrated gem of a little loved and only faintly remembered era and scene—the moment when 'Blackie Clueless', as some of the wits of contemporary music criticism had it, dug deep enough to come out with some genuinely disturbed material. If part of what we learned was that those depths were not always very deep (cock rocker in 'not super-engaged with the world' shocker!) let's not overlook the greater lesson—that on his day, Blackie could scale significant heights of lyric writing, with subject matter that went beyond how much he liked having a dick and using it, and in doing so created an album that while undeniably flawed, stands as both a significant achievement in its own right, and a signpost for a lyrical approach in metal that was then far less travelled, and infinitely more interesting, than what almost everyone else was doing.

Also, you know, it's a horror album. The soundtrack to what in 1987 looked like the most plausible cause of the apocalypse. It captured that mood so well it still has the ability to reach its rotting arms across the decades between, and chill you just a little with its touch. It's a ghost of a ghost, but still has the power to haunt.

No small achievement.

MY BRIEF CAREER AS AN ELEVEN-YEAR-OLD SLAVE TRADER

It's my final summer of primary school. And depending on when it fell, I'm either ten or eleven. But it's been elevens all round so far, so let's suppose that's right for this too. At a certain point it seems like synchronicity has its own gravitational pull, and the notion that many of my biggest formative intellectual and artistic experiences came within a couple of months of turning eleven pleases me.

So we'll suppose I'm eleven, waiting out my final year of primary school, and looking forward with a naivety that is still heartbreaking even this far out to secondary school, where I am assured by adults who should really have known differently that there things will be taken Much More Seriously, where I will be Appropriately Stretched, and where they do not tolerate Mucking About. And yes that last point should have given me pause, but these were respected adult voices, people whose words I trusted implicitly, so I assumed that 'mucking about' meant 'bullying' and not, say, 'having fun.'

Oh to be eleven again.

So the slow tick-tock of the dog days of summer term (prior to the start of summer proper) grind down, slow and sure and fine. That's how it should have gone.

MY BRIEF CAREER AS AN ELEVEN-YEAR-OLD...

Instead, something happens.

That something is a new trainee teacher, who is specialising in drama (the subject, she didn't create emotional strife wherever she went, or at least not in the classroom). Somehow this poor lady had drawn the shortest possible straw, and been sent out to the ass end of North Devon to try and teach Drama to a bunch of yokels and farmers sons and daughters, for most of whom the height of sophisticated performance art is doing impersonations of what they imagine people of Indian or Pakistani descent must sound like, which are so shockingly poor and horrendously racist that even Spike 'put it in the curry' Milligan would have probably shaken his head and muttered something about taking it too far and ruining it for everyone. And if that sounds like a fun time, I assure you, I'm telling it wrong.

This poor woman; exactly who the department for education she'd pissed off enough to get this assignment, I cannot imagine. Nor can I adequately picture what offence can have led to such a dire assignment. But luckily for me, she didn't seem to give a single solitary shit about any of that. Instead, she rolled up her sleeves and jumped in with both feet (meaning she got her boots wet, and if you spotted that, award yourself an invisible calorie free doughnut, on me).

The current topic for our history classes was the slave trade. The head of the school, who also ran the classroom for nine, ten and eleven year olds (yup, two years of teaching in a single classroom, and still less than thirty kids—and yes, same chap as from the *Appetite* essay), loved teaching history. It made sense. After all, if your prime source of pleasure comes from instilling terror into the minds of young pupils and torturing them psychologically from a position of authority, you can scarcely conceive of a more perfect subject than the history of our species.

In the eighteen months since I'd joined the class, I'd learned about the various torture and execution regimes of kings and queens past (being hung, drawn and quartered seemed particularly and spectacularly gruesome, although it occurred to me even then that there was a good chance that unless you had some exceptional fortitude, you were unlikely to make it very far into the actual quartering stage, what with the pain and blood loss). We'd had the rack and the wheel, burnings and beheadings (did you know that kings had to be executed with a sword rather than an axe because it was a 'noble' weapon? Maybe, but I'm betting less of you knew because you were taught, *at eleven years old,* that this was one of the few times nobility was a bit of a bummer, because the curved blade of an axe would normally remove a head with one clean stroke, whereas even the sharpest of swords wielded by the strongest of men would take several hacking strokes to fully remove the head. You'd be alive through the entire process and feel each blow. Yes, that level of detail. The youngest members of the class were nine). We'd learned about how certain medieval kings would force people who displeased them into iron cages small enough that they had to crouch, then simply hang them outside the castle walls and let nature take its course. Birds would often eat their eyes before they died, I was informed. The bodies would be left there as they rotted to skeletons. As a warning to others.

Anything else? Oh, indeed. The Dark Ages were a particularly rich source of learning material, what with the many lethal trials that would either kill an innocent woman or identify a witch (that particular Python sketch never quite rocked my world the way it did many of my contemporaries, I suspect, but that's the power of teaching for you). It wasn't just women who got a raw deal though. Can't decide if you're telling the truth? Plunge your hand into the boiling water to retrieve the stone at the bottom. Assuming you don't either drop the stone or pass out from the pain (both clear and unarguable signifiers of guilt) your arm is bandaged for a week before being unwrapped and examined. If you're healing normally, congrats, you were telling the truth, you get to live, albeit with a scarred and damaged arm and hand. Show any sign of infection, though, and oh dear, you fibber, time to have a body part amputated.

I've looked none of this up to check—I'm on a boat and the internet is £300 a minute and crap, and I don't fucking need to. It's burned into my brain, horror upon horror, brutality and sadism and mass cruelty. All true, all real, no werewolves or vampires required. Just people, doing unto others whatever the hell they want with no consequence—indeed, with the full approval and mark of authority, which I think is what scared me the most; insanity and brutality was not just tolerated, it was fucking mandated. Good as 1984 is, I think the reason it didn't have the universe shifting impact on me as it did on many young minds was the simple fact that by the time I'd gotten to it, I'd already fully absorbed and internalised the idea that unchecked authority would quickly lead to scarily high levels of violence, sadism and insanity. It's one of the most basic and disturbing truths about our species, one I struggle with and fear and write about to this day.

You want to know what hell looks like? Check out North Korea, check out Nazi Germany, check out Soviet Russia, check out Ghengis Kahn sometime, check out medieval Europe. Take a good long hard look at what we do to each other when we let might and might alone be the arbiter of right and wrong. Look it up.

While you're there, check out the slave trade.

As you may imagine from the above, fertile ground for our head teacher. His particular delight was lurid descriptions of the conditions on board the boats: we were given the photocopied diagrams that showed the number of people per deck, impossible totals, stick figures arranged like jigsaw pieces, but which did little to convey the visceral horror of the real conditions. But lucky old us, because we had Sir, and Sir was more than equal to the task of transmitting that terror into our minds.

The smells, of vomit and shit, all evacuations left where they fell, the decks washed down maybe once a week with seawater. Women crying, men calling out for loved ones. The chains and manacles, biting into flesh, raw wounds that the seawater would attack, inflame, sometimes infect. Exposure to white man's diseases, which would often prove fatal on the voyage. Truly meagre rations of food and water, many more dying of starvation (or, more commonly, dehydration). Massive brutality and violence meted out at the slightest provocation, real or imagined. The raw terror of minute-to-minute existence, ripped from everything you could call home, family, tribe, society. Anything you knew or could count on. Chained and floating towards an unknown destination, the only clue to your final fate being your bonds and the cruelty of your captors.

'Some of them just gave up. They just willed themselves to die on the boat.'

I'll say this for the vicious, brutal, sadistic old fuck—I never got the slightest whiff of racism from him in any of this. Certainly my abiding and overriding memory of the lessons is a sense of gut revulsion at the awfulness of the experience of being chained in that hold, and he did nothing to alleviate or mitigate that. Which may mean nothing more than his enjoying our discomfort, but it's still something, given the time and place. I contextualize that because of what follows, which those familiar with the work of Neil Gaiman will already be familiar with, but which again had a much more blunted impact on me when I read it in the pages of *Sandman* at seventeen because I'd been told it in school when I was fucking *eleven*.

Because as improbable as it may seem to those unfamiliar with the period and process, there was actually a grotesque punchline to the above, a truly macabre kicker, which was this: all the slaves in each deck were chained to each other in one continuous link. Because for the British fleets, slave trading was illegal, and if they got caught with a cargo full of contraband, things were apt to get sticky. So at the other end of the interlinked chains was a huge stone weight. At the first sign of customs boats, the weight would simply be dropped overboard, dragging the entire contents of the boat—that would be several hundred human beings—down to the seabed.

Profit margins on illegal slave trading were so huge, I was informed, that they could afford to dump six out of every seven 'shipments' and still make a tidy return.

I don't know about sleepless nights, exactly, but I think it's fair to say it haunted me, and haunts me still, given the level of recall on a subject I've ostensibly not thought about for years, if not decades. It's a cliché, but some knowledge, some information really does seem to carry emotional weight. It's in my nature to want to know, to seek out and learn and digest and try to make sense of things, and it's been an enriching journey so far, but every now and again, you will come across something like this, and just be sat firmly on your arse for a while.

Enter our trainee drama teacher.

Because there's a ton you could do, given the subject matter. And let's face facts, most of it would be pretty shit. Luckily for us, we got sent a genius.

'On Friday afternoon, instead of normal lessons, we're going to do a special project on the slave trade. We're going to enact an international court trying to make a decision about whether or not the slave trade should be made illegal.'

To say my ears pricked up would be an understatement. I was mesmerised.

'You'll each be assigned roles, based on the different historical interests involved, and have to give testimony and argue for or against the trade. At the end will be a vote to decide if the trade should be ended.'

I don't know if it was Tuesday or Wednesday. I just know the week couldn't go by soon enough. I was stoked. I think even at eleven I knew I was pretty good at marshalling and sustaining an argument, but what an opportunity I had here! I started making plans, rehearsing rhetoric. I was going to wax lyrical about injustice, about the cruelty of the conditions, I was going to invoke biblical quotes, I was going to kick ass. By the time I was done talking, the slave trade would be abolished by unanimous consent. Probably we'd all get sent home early.

Following lunch, we all lined up to go back to class, my tummy fluttering with more than just the effects of toffee sponge and pink custard. The classroom had been rearranged, one huge long table with the trainee sat at one end, playing the judge, and cards with our names on so we knew where to sit. I remember being close to the judge, and sat next to Sir, who was also participating, but can recall not a single warning bell as I sat in my place, all but cracking my knuckles in anticipation.

'Blah-blah, international court blah-blah, gathered here blah-blah, interested parties blah-blah, resolve whether or not slavery should be abolished.'

Game *on*!

'Now, turn over your name cards to see the role you've been assigned.'

I'm not even kidding, I read the word 'Slave', and actually had time to feel a swell of pride before I read the second word.

Which was, of course, 'Trader'.

I remember looking up at the trainee, not quite tears in the eyes, but definitely with no small measure of hurt. Why would she do this to me? How could she not know how I felt?

Wise woman. She knew exactly what she was doing.

'I know it'll be hard, Kit, but try.'

There was a final twist of the knife, of course. We were seated by role, so the fact that I was sat next to Sir meant he was the other assigned trader. Meaning we would have to work together.

It was crushing.

At first.

Then, as the opening testimonies began, I started to see... possibilities. It dawned on me, quickly, that it was possible I could have an enormous amount of fun with this. Because, dig it: I knew where I actually stood morally, but I also knew the now-opposing argument like the back of my hand. As the weight of the emotion of the whole horror show dropped from me, as I confronted the scenario not as articulating a passionately held belief but simply putting forward the strongest argument for a position, I realised this was something I could not just do, but enjoy doing. In the process, I hit on one of the great truths of acting, and maybe even of make believe and fiction in general.

It's *always* more fun to play the bad guy.

And I played it to the hilt. I talked about civilizing influence, the gainful employment of the ship crews, the appalling conditions we were rescuing these people from and the relatively prosperous circumstances they were being transported to, even as slaves. I flat-out denied the cruelties of the voyage, blaming any losses as a weakness within an inferior species, and you'd better believe I quoted biblical justification for slavery. By the time I'd finished, the girl who'd set herself up as chief spokesperson for the slaves was damn near in tears of anger and outrage at the mendacious eloquence coming out of me (we were friends afterwards though, once the heat of battle had died away—she got theatre too).

I had a ball. I had a blast. I rocked it and socked it. For one glorious afternoon, I was an eleven-year-old slave trader, and it was some of the most fun I've had in a classroom.

POSTSCRIPT (*Or, What Have We Learned?*):

Because obviously, as a human being with a conscience, I can't leave it there. Even with two and a half thousand words of context, that final paragraph is pretty shocking. So, 'enjoyed' how? And to what end?

I think part of what we are talking about here is the power of play, right? For all that the head teacher delighted in traumatising us with the horror of the industry, the one insight that couldn't give me, the one perspective I could never grasp, was that of the men who plied and profited from this trade. It was incomprehensible to me that someone would be responsible for such cruelty... until I came to inhabit that person, in play.

Then, the scales fell quickly. Because *of course*, if you profit from a system, you'll find a way to justify its perpetuation. *Of course*, you'll find a way to render the status quo not merely legal, but ethical, even righteous. *Of course* you'll minimise, deflect, deny and obfuscate any sense of fallout or human consequences of what you do.

Because that's what power does.

It would be a long time before the concept of 'privilege' would cross my radar, in the context of gender and ethnicity debates, but I had zero problems with conceptualising it as soon as it came along, because I'd felt the power of it. Aged eleven, in a classroom of my peers, I had donned the mantle of privilege and used it to justify horrific barbarity.

That alone made it worth the price of admission. To this day, whenever I find myself reading the news, or studying history, and I also find myself saying/thinking, 'I just can't imagine how a person could...' I stop myself, mid-expression. Because thanks to that lesson, I often find that, with just a bit of thought, I *can*. It's one of the reasons I write the kind of fiction that I write: Because, with just a little effort, I can imagine why or how a person *could*... and I feel like those stories are worth telling. Also, because I think the biggest disservice we do ourselves, as a species, is to monster the bad people, to claim them as other, as inhuman. No matter how vile the person and how offensive the crime, the hard truth is that they *are* always human. We ignore or forget that at our peril, because I'm pretty sure that the only way to truly contend with and ultimately defeat evil in the world is to understand it.

Know thine enemy.

That said, there's also the less palatable, uncomfortable part of the privilege aspect, which is that this lesson/exercise was probably only possible in an all-white classroom. Even in the bygone age of 1989, I simply cannot imagine assigning a black child frankly any of the roles in this process without generating an utterly righteous shitstorm that would have caused a flurry of P45's all round—and, to be clear, quite right too.

And that's—to put it mildly—a problem. Because an educational experience that's exclusionary on grounds of race is instinctively an anathema to me, I hope for obvious reasons.

And yet. I learned so much.

I don't really have an answer, but I will say this: people of colour are not responsible for racism, and they can't solve it. We know this, because, as the primary victims of racism and racist culture, if they could fix it, they would have. No, the burden, the responsibility, of rejecting racism has ultimately to rest with white people. We started it, we perpetuate it, and only we can ultimately stop it. We can, should, and must elevate, listen to, and learn from, black voices on this subject, for sure; but ultimately, we white folk have to shoulder responsibility for finding a way to just stop.

It feels instinctively counterintuitive, if not outright wrong, to suggest that an all-white classroom finding ways to explore racism could possibly be part of the solution. That *can't* be right. There must be—there will be—a better way.

But for me, it was certainly part of the story of my journey to becoming an antiracist; more, a pivotal, scales-from-the-eyes moment. As such, it's a moment I will always feel grateful for.

PPS—We lost the debate handily, by seven votes to twenty-one, and slavery was abolished (the aboriginal land rights vote a month later went right down to the wire, but that's a story for another day). All the boat crews voted against the trade, doing themselves out of jobs in the process. Which has a kind of nobility at this distance, though I remember feeling pissed about it at the time.

SECONDARY YEARS

12 – 16

ASSUME AN ATTITUDE

Bring Your Daughter to the Slaughter

It's December 30th, 1990. A Sunday. I am twelve. One year after *IT*, slave trading, and *Appetite For Destruction*. I'm in North Devon, on the top floor of a large house in the tiny village I call home. Christmas is Dad time, but Christmas is done, and we're back in the sticks. Depending on how long I've been back, I've probably already had my first back-from-dad's-house row with my sister. It's the day before New Year's Eve. And it's 4pm, so my obsession with music compels me to sit in my bedroom, radio/cassette tuned to BBC Radio 1, record and pause buttons depressed.

It's Top 40 time.

This is a relatively new obsession, and a relatively short lived one, too. It won't be long until the crashing drums and screaming guitars banish chart music from my soul for good, exorcised permanently by the high priests of rock and metal—but for now, just for now, I have one foot on each side of the divide, perhaps best typified by the aforementioned C90 cassette I own that contains a pirate copy of Skid Row's debut on side A, and New Kids On The Block's *Hangin' Tough* on side B. I still attend the under-eighteen discos at the youth centre in the local town, on occasion, and if you're going to dance, you have to know the tunes. Interesting that looking back I wasn't ashamed to dance, which as anyone who has seen me dance will tell you is... odd. But there were older girls there, and I was short enough to be cute, and they liked it when I danced. So I danced.

Anyway.

In August 1991, there will be a moment at the end of an episode of MTV's Headbangers Ball when Lonn Friend will hold up two 'album of the month' choices—three, actually. That moment will, in retrospect, represent a perfect changing of the guard (as well as the death of shows like Headbangers Ball). The recommendations are *Use Your Illusion I* and *II*, and *Nevermind*. But that's seven long months away. Right now, in 1990, we're still waiting on a new Guns N' Roses album, Raw magazine is the fortnightly alternative to *Kerrang!*, and in a tiny village in North Devon, I sit with my tape recorder poised, waiting to see what will happen.

The first thing of note for me will have been The Proclaimers cover of 'King Of The Road,' hanging on at number 40. To be honest, I still think that's a pretty good tune, though I couldn't say this specific version has stuck.

I don't remember Black Box's 'Fantasy' at 39, but 'Ride On Time' was a floor filler, so I may well have recorded it. The rest of the top 30 is at best forgettable, at worst... I mean, Rod Stewart and Tina Turner—'It Takes Two'? 'Geordie Boys (Gazza Rap)' by Gazza? I've had the fucking time of my motherfucking life? My ears bleed from the memory. Talk about horror.

ASSUME AN ATTITUDE

Was I waiting for a reason? Did I know what was coming? I just can't remember. It's possible.

30 to 20 doesn't fare much better—a lot of Christmas tunes plummeting now silly season is done. I might have been tempted in by 'Kinky Boots', but probably not. Definitely not INXS. But then, new in at number 23... Anthrax, 'Got The Time'.

And I mean, fucking hell kids, you should go give this one a spin right now. I'll wait.

Within the year I will hear this song live. At what I have only just remembered was my first actual live gig—not The Pixies at Exeter University, the gig I tell everyone is my first, the one I remember as my first. This one takes place in a school. I can't remember which—not mine. But it's a school band, called Killing Time, and it's their last ever show, because school's out and they're all off to college or work. So it's summer 1991, logically. I'm smoking by then, at least part time, which is younger than I remember. I have three or four straights that I'd purloined or purchased somewhere and stored in a cassette tape case, and I let some girl my friend and I met at the gig smoke most of them, before cluing in that she was only into me for my nicotine and going off in a sulk. I sulk through most of the support act and the main event. I'm wearing my Metallica T-shirt. Yes, because the girl who's the singer for the headline band sees it as I'm checking out the support band, points and laughs good naturedly, miming someone playing a heavy guitar, her grunge sensibilities clearly amused by my 'dinosaurs of rock' stylings, and I laugh and shrug. But...

Hang on. If I'm wearing my Metallica shirt, it can't be 1991. I got that shirt at the '93 MK Bowl show, the *Nowhere Else To Roam* tour. And if it's a summer holiday gig, it has to be the summer after that. Which means I didn't hear this song live until I was fifteen, which explains why the girl part bothered me so much and also means that The Pixies really were my first live band.

Phew. That got scary for a second.

Okay, take two: four years later, I'll hear this song live. The band, Killing Time, will do their set, and a dickhead in an Anthrax T-shirt will headbang all through the show, impressing the hell out of the girl who smoked my cigarettes, in the process earning my undying enmity. The band end the set and get an encore, and the guy with the Anthrax T-shirt will request this song, and the band, after apologizing 'to anyone who's ever known us,' launch into a funk cover version that gets everyone dancing, before a straight up cover that tears the lid off the place, and gets me headbanging like it was my idea all along. I'll spend most of the evening back at my friend's house hurling my guts up, probably a result of passively smoking half the weed in the hall, but right in the moment the band play that song, this song, I am having a total blast. It worked amazingly well with a female vocal, too.

TL;DR—I have a deep personal connection with this song that obliterates any pretence at objectivity, but I still think it's bloody amazing. I recorded and replayed the hell out of it, and spent the rest of the chart convinced I'd landed my prize.

Into the top twenty, and it's back to slim pickings;

Chris Isaak, Jive fucking Bunny (if you don't know, look it up; or, better, don't), Status Quo, New Kids, more Black Box. 'Unchained Melody'? A Levi commercial, maybe? Hell if I know. Had made number one, now on the way down. Number twelve I vividly remember recording—'Unbelievable', by EMF. Dirty secret? I still think it's a pretty good song—especially the live version with the guitar front and centre. Don't judge, especially if you're a Lost Boys fan (see next essay). And number eleven was 'Crazy', by Seal, a song I remember admiring for the vocal, even though the tune was not my thing. It's also interesting how many of these songs were still around the top 20 on 27th January, 1991—but that's another story (one for two essays time).

The top ten awaits. Passingly unlikely that I'll get anything else good, but I've come this far, so what the hell? Only killing time anyway.

Did I know? I really don't think I did, but maybe... maybe...

10—'Pray', MC Hammer. Bill Hicks has my proxy on this, though I danced to it at the time, no doubt. 8—Madonna, 'Justify My Love'. The video didn't translate well to radio. I still probably dug it. 7—'All Together Now', The Farm. I cannot explain to you why this song still gets to me, but it does. 6—'You've Lost That Lovin' Feelin''—okay, when we're done I need to look up what the fuck this and 'Unchained Melody' were doing competing in the UK singles chart for Christmas 1990, because that's bizarre.

(Morgan Freeman narrator: 'In fact, he never did look it up, and the mystery remains, one Google

search away from solving. Such is the life of the cultural magpie.')

Top five now. 'The Grease Megamix'. Enya. Cliff Richard's annual Christmas cash grab is still in the top 3. And number 2 is Vanilla Ice with 'Ice Ice Baby'. Yeah, probably I did.

And then, with practiced sadism, the DJ reads out the entire chart again before announcing the number 1. A new entry.

Iron Maiden had form, that's the thing. 'Holy Smoke' had come out in September and made the Top 3. I'd recorded that off the radio, you'd better believe it, and listened to it over and over, trying to figure out the lyrics. Scott, still a metalhead at that age, still seven glorious months before *Levelling The Land* and *Nevermind* tore a musical rift between us, proudly showed me the CD picture disk single, featuring typically amazing artwork. And, you know, of the two singles, it's almost certainly the better song—smarter, sharper. I've been listening to the two tunes back to back as I write (with a brief Anthrax sojourn) and yeah, 'Holy Smoke' is a stonker; I'm not wild about the intro, but the verse has that trademark take-no-prisoners Maiden stomp, and the chorus lead lick is a simple but pleasing hook. And for those of us who care about such things, it's a pretty sharp lyric too—sure, Televangelists are hardly a tough target, but that doesn't make them less worthy of ridicule—and of course Maiden had a fair share of their own albums burned by this point, so, you know, they had skin in the game.

None of which quite explains how it made number

3 in the singles chart. That took a little something extra—mainly strategy. The single was released in September, on no less than six formats (CD picture disk, 12' picture disk, cassette, 7' single, the works), with a blitz advertising campaign in the metal press—they went for it. And when it happened, it was pretty stunning—one of 'my' bands in the top 5, blasting metal at all the pop pretenders. Pretty sweet.

Turns out, that was the test run.

Because it also turns out that the slowest week for singles sales is Christmas week. Makes sense—the Christmas number 1 has been settled, and nobody wants to brave the shops.

No one but Iron Maiden fans.

'So here it is; a brand new entry at number 1— Iron Maiden—"Bring Your Daughter To The Slaughter!"' The DJ sounds like he can't quite believe it. Probably he can't. Radio 1 had just issued a blanket ban on Maiden, effectively declaring them to be irrelevant relics (think about that alongside still playing Cliff Richard and see what it does for your blood pressure). But no one told Maiden, no one told Maiden *fans*, and in a big house in a tiny village in North Devon, a lonely twelve-year-old metalhead is grinning fit to split. It's a bloody miracle.

Iron Maiden is number 1, and all's right with the world.

And sure '...Daughter' is hardly a classic Maiden song, and it's from what's generally regarded the weakest Dickinson record, but... well, two things.

One, it may not be classic Maiden, but it is *quintessential* Maiden. All the elements you might want are present and correct—horror movie imagery in the lyrics (courtesy of the song's origins as a Dickinson solo track for *Elm Street 5*, a movie we shall return to in *Volume II*), stomping verses, a crunching chorus, decent solo and middle eight—it's representative, and though I know many fans disagree, I was never embarrassed by it.

Two—it's fucking number 1. Iron Maiden did it, and they did it without selling out in the normal sense—no fluffy ballad, no shit hot music video. No, they did it by a combination of ruthless strategy and mass mobilisation of their fan base.

There were complaints, including letters to the editor accusing the charts of being rigged. A gang of bikers drove down to BBC television studio with a giant Eddie in toe and a petition to get Maiden air play again. But the truth was, by then they didn't need it. They'd proved they could beat the mainstream without joining it or compromising.

You really don't have to like Maiden to recognise the singular contribution they've made to Metal in general, and British Metal in particular. In a week where the world rightly mourns the passing of another metal legend (*this refers to the passing of Motorhead frontman and legend Lemmy, who died the week this was written*), it's worth reflecting on the band that are arguably only second to Sabbath in their influence and stature over a global genre of music.

So there's that. And sure, they're headlining Download 2016, and I can't wait to see them doing their thing.

But for all that, I can't deny that they'll never mean more to me than they did on 30th December

1990. They achieved the impossible and did it like the Monkey King—they invaded heaven and brought it crashing down around them. And then, grinning, strode off to conquer the world.

Up the Irons.

KILL YOUR BROTHER, YOU'LL FEEL BETTER

The Lost Boys

Because here's the thing—sometimes you go back, and it's bad. Not just 'not as good as I remember,' not just 'hasn't aged well,' I'm talking 'actively god-awful, what the hell was I thinking, now I hate myself and the decade of my youth just a little more than I did before' bad.

Back when I talked about the W.A.S.P. record *The Headless Children*, I noted how the album essentially broke down into three camps in terms of the individual songs, those camps being 'actually, that's still a legitimately good song,' 'that's obviously not great but I remember why I liked it' and 'how did I *ever* think that was an acceptable use of my time?'

But what to do when an entire artifact falls into that final camp? How do you approach it when you have a film that's a no-brainer shoe-in for *My Life In Horror*—a movie that honesty dictates you must include, that was formative and hugely influential on thirteen-year-old you—but also one that you saw more recently and detested? Despised? Flat out hated? Disliked so much you felt ashamed of the young you, and the holes in his critical thinking and

KILL YOUR BROTHER, YOU'LL FEEL BETTER

evaluation that were so large a garbage truck like this could be driven through?

Tonight, I will attempt to provide an answer to that question. Tonight, armed only with a netbook, a bottle of Bulleit Bourbon, a tin Deadwood shot glass, a packet of Tunnock's Caramel wafer biscuits, and a copy of the movie, I will attempt to channel thirteen-year-old me. Talk to him, but also have him talk through me. Reason with him, in the unlikely event that such a thing is possible. Tonight, I aim to put that little goober straight, while also giving him the chance to make his tragically misguided case. A transcript of a commentary track recorded across time, if you will.

Wish me luck.

It's time to talk about *The Lost Boys*.

Old Kit: See, it's not even started and I'm being trolled. Sky Movies Greats? That's the channel they chose to broadcast this cinematic abortion? Was the schedule on 'Sky Movies Nostalgic But Shit' all full up with Tango and Cash reruns?

Young Kit: Sky clearly knows more about good movies than you do.

OK: Shut up kid, I'm trying to watch this crap.

OK: Five seconds in, and the drum and synth combination already make this irredeemable.

directed by Joel Schumacher appears on screen

OK: Prosecution rests, Yer Honor.

YK: You've got issues, man.

OK: The gang looks like an MTV director's idea of what a group of rockers actually looks like.

YK: I think they look cool.

OK: I can't believe I used to be you. Is that the shittiest cold open in the history of movies? Manages to simultaneously destroy any sense of mystery about if the gang are vampires, while still pretending to be coy. What's the point? Terrible storytelling.

'People Are Strange' plays, OK hits Pause

OK: Okay, this. This right here. This is the fucking problem with this whole shitty movie, expressed clearly in a single song choice over-montage. Everything that is facile, surface and putrid about this film is summed up right here.

YK: What the hell, man? It's a fucking great song. When the guy sees the 'murder capital of the world' on the back of the road sign and shit, it fits really well. What's your problem?

OK: My problem, dipstick, is that the song was originally written and performed by The Doors, one of the most iconic bands of the 60s counterculture. It was originally written as an anthem of dispossession and alienation, expressing a zeitgeist of profound generational disconnect and mutual antagonism that genuinely seemed to be tearing the fabric of the country apart, sung by an alcoholic, chronically shy poet who also thought he was The Lizard King and would invoke the spirit of Dionysus on stage while performing.

YK: So?

OK: So that version of the song exists and in its place we've got Echo and the *fucking* Bunnymen covering it. I ask you, who in the history of the human species has *ever* listened to both versions of this song and thought, 'Yeah, no, let's go with The Bunnymen version—it's a little... cleaner?' I'll fucking tell you who...

YK: Erm, Joel Schumacher?

OK: Joel *fucking* Schumacher. That one vapid, tepid, sterile choice tells you everything that's wrong about what's to come. It's a fucking travesty. The whole thing. And here at the six-minute marker, we know all we need to.

YK: Okay, but can we actually watch the film now? Because I'm not getting any younger.

OK: Smartass.

roll tape

OK: Missing kids posters. Wow, subtle.

YK: 'Nothin' legal!' *Love* that line!

OK: Missing kids posters too subtle? Don't worry, here's more! How fucking dumb do they think we are? Also, literally every single person in this film has bad hair.

YK: 'You know what it means when there's no TV? No MTV!' Come on man, that's funny.

OK: I hate you so much.

OK: Are we supposed to suspect the old man in some way? And that line about all the corpses standing up would apply to any town or city of any size on the fucking planet. God this movie is dumb. And how old is Michael supposed to be? Any younger than thirty, we've got a problem.

OK: Oh God, the oiled sax player on the beach. I can't watch.

YK: What? It's cool.

OK: It's a rock concert directed by someone who's never, ever been to a rock concert. Or liked rock music. There's people headbanging! To a saxophone. So dumb.

YK: You're an uptight guy, you know that? That video store looks awesome. As does the comic shop.

OK: I'll give you that. But what the actual fuck is Feldman wearing?

Frog brother describes Feldman as a 'fashion victim'

OK: God fucking damnit!

YK: *laughing hysterically* You know nothing, Old Kit! This movie is smarter than you!

OK: The Frog brothers are not enough to redeem this atrocity of a movie. But they are so far the only remotely watchable part. That bit where the girl got onto Jack Bauer's bike, on the other hand, was shot like a bad Bruce Springsteen video from the 80s.

YK: I wouldn't know.

OK: Fuck you.

YK: That old guy is hysterical.

OK: That old guy is filler. Bad, pointless filler.

OK: Okay, I realise this is bordering on a cheap shot, given the era, but how is Star a functioning character on any level? As opposed to an object of desire? Granted this is only her second or third scene (and tellingly the first one where she gets any lines) but do any of her actions or statements in this entire movie work on any level approaching consistency or internal logic?

YK: How fucking cool is that line? 'You don't have to beat me Michael. You just have to try and keep up'?

OK: Precisely zero cool. And it plunges into anti-cool once the soundtrack kicks in for the bike race.

YK: Do you not like fun, or something?

YK: I wish I had a hangout like the Lost Boys. Look at that place.

OK: Shut *up*. Oh God, it's the noodles scene. Oh, but not before *another* entirely pointless scene with Feldman and grandpa. Is this movie a million hours long?

YK: Well, if you keep pausing it... Oh, maggots!

OK: 'They're only noodles, Michael.' I just got eyestrain from rolling them. And why does Michael even want to be in this lame ass gang? It makes one-hundred per cent no sense. And there's a *fucking* Jim Morrison picture on the *actual* wall of the vampire hangout, are you taking the *fucking* piss?

YK: Why do you care so much? Were you *in* the fucking Doors or something? I mean, you look old enough...

OK: Listen you little shit...

YK: Shh! I like this bit!

OK: Well, why wouldn't you? It's like someone described psychedelia to someone who'd never touched drugs, then that person directed someone else who'd also never done it to...

YK: Not that bit! This bit. The bridge bit.

OK: Why? Because the idiot headbangs for *no reason*?

YK: No, because it's cool man, he thinks he's gonna die...

OK: If fucking only. And he ends up back on his bed... how? And why does he go under the bridge in the first place? I mean, I get he's not that bright, but come on. I'd also like to point out that we're almost one third of the way through the running time of this movie, and almost nothing has happened, and none of what has happened has made any sense, and there has been exactly one funny line. Can I go to bed yet?

YK: Sure. I'll stay up and drink your whiskey.

OK: The hell you will... Man, Michael really cannot act at all, can he? I mean, he's a plank.

YK: Shh! Corey is singing along with that song in the bath! That falsetto is *so* funny.

OK: He's literally the only thirteen-year-old in America who knows the words to that song. This is so dumb.

YK: He wakes up on the ceiling. That. Is. Awesome.

OK: It's a nice idea, utterly ruined by Michael's inability to do anything other than gurn.

YK: That bit where he picks up the phone while floating out the window... so funny.

OK: Kid, you don't know what funny is. You're out of your element. I also don't buy Sam's flip-flop here *at all*. It's that classic fault with a lot of horror movies that relies on people basically being as stupid as possible for the plot to progress. Gah, I hate that so much.

YK: It's supposed to be funny!

OK: But Garlic in cloves don't smell. It's the most basic reality fail.

YK: Were you ever young?

OK: Fuck off. Oh lord, shitty 'sex' scene alert...

YK: Okay, yeah, even I have to admit this bit is bad.

OK: I may have mentioned it before, but this soundtrack is awful.

YK: It's not that bad.

OK: Shut up. Get back to me after you've seen *The Crow*, okay? And I love how flying outside his brother's window is no problem, but the magical healing dog bite throws him for a loop? Dumb, dumb, dumb.

YK: That bit with the dog is so cool.

OK: Pfft. 'Kill your brother. You'll feel better' is a good line though. But are the Frog brothers meant to be delusional sad sacks who just happen to be right, or actual real vampire hunters? The fucking script flip-flops almost line by line. In related news, how can you not tell the difference between grated parmesan and fucking garlic?

YK: It's a great scene though. The way the tests each fail spectacularly, and Max's little riff on 'not trying to replace your father.' It's fun. Do you even remember fun?

OK: Shh! It's the one decent song on the whole soundtrack. You can almost hear it underneath the shitty dialogue. That also has to be the lamest, tamest mass murder ever committed to film.

YK: It's not supposed to be scary, dickhead! It's supposed to be fun. See? A closet full of stuffed animals. Hilarious.

OK: Funny like small pox. Why is he hiding under a duvet cover? Garlic? Holy water? Ring a bell, pillock?

YK: Ooh, the first staking! Come on, you've got to admit this bit is cool.

OK: Man, even the fucking Frog brothers are getting on my tits now. They're so... 'wacky'. Bleugh. And is this supposed to be tense or atmospheric? It's just so damn slow. And I'm really supposed to think either Frog is physically strong enough to drive a lump of wood clear through a vampire with *one hand*? Do vampires have rib cages made out of cardboard? Because if not...

YK: Do I really grow up to be such a pedantic killjoy? Look, his hand caught fire in the sun! Outstanding!

OK: Boy, was I easily pleased. Wow, that Plan A/Plan B dialogue was tortured.

YK: I know you meant to say brilliant. And I love this bit with the font water.

OK: Oh God, it's the 'big fight build up' montage. Because we haven't ticked enough cliché boxes. And I love how when your vampire mate is murdered, you just go back to sleep until sundown. Also, could they not afford effects shots of the vampires flying or what?

YK: This is a good scene with Max and Feldman's mum.

OK: She's a great actress. She deserved better. Also, this Frog dialogue is dumb—we just saw them totally shit the bed after staking one vampire, and now they're giving it all, 'it's never a pretty sight.' You may search in vain for consistency.

YK: Will you shut up? You're missing the dog chase bit.

OK: Spoilers: they make it back to the house.

YK: Shut *up*! Okay, I defy you to tell me that bit where the vampire explodes out of the fireplace isn't cool.

OK: Pfft. It's all right, but so what? And this fucking dialogue. 'You Killed Marco!' 'Yeah, and you're next!' 'No, you're next!'

YK: It's supposed to be funny!

OK: It fucking isn't. Can't they all die, somehow? That'd be funny. Still, at least the Stephen Adler lookalike can go back to… wait, why is blood exploding out of all the plumbing? It makes *no sense*!

YK: It's *supposed to be funny*! This bit is awesome. The bow and arrow, fake out miss, 'Only once pal'—'Death by stereo!'

OK: Kill me now. Better yet, kill you.

YK: Here we go, the big standoff.

OK: Did that Frog brother really just call Feldman 'Sambo'? This film is profoundly odd in places. And that was some unforgivable use of slo-mo right there.

YK: Oh hush. This is a great scrap.

OK: 'My blood is in your veins!' 'So is mine!' This is unforgivably poor. And now the shitty music and lingering smoke… no, no, no. This is everything that's bad about music videos of the era, and it's in a bloody movie. God, I'm so depressed.

YK: Here we go. Here comes Max. Fucking brilliant.

OK: It's a good performance; I'll give you that. It's still a dumb twist though. Like, if he really wanted what he says he wanted, he could have had it on page 20 of the script. Stupid, stupid, stupid…

YK: Here's Grandpa!

OK: And just when you thought the shark couldn't be more jumped, here, as you say, comes Grandpa. You do realise there is no reason at all for him to drive his truck into his own fucking living room? None, nada, before or after the scene. It happens just because the script needs it to happen. And as if to underline the point, it's back to the shitty, inferior *People Are Strange* cover for the end credits. Yup, that was every bit as underwhelming and woeful an experience as I remember it.

YK: It's a fun movie. There are some great action sequences, good makeup and effects. Some really funny lines. I'm sure it'll hold up just fine.

Well, there you have it, the Kit Power-across-time commentary track for Lost Boys. One thing's for sure—barring some truly extraordinary set of circumstances, I am done with this godforsaken movie for the rest of my life. I guess for that alone I'll have to call this a win. Still. Let's never do this ever again.

POSTSCRIPT: The morning after.

Because I have to be honest, that wasn't as much fun as I'd expected. Part of that may be down to the fact that I peaked early (at the six minute mark, to be precise, for those keeping score at home). But I think a lot of it is that the last time I saw this movie three or four years ago, I actively hated it, and I'd just expected my reaction to be the same, and it… wasn't. Maybe it was the presence of thirteen-year-old me, or maybe it was simple recalibration. That first rewatch, I'd sat with a head full of great memories, and then the movie just took a big shit all over them. This time… yeah, this time, expectations were basically grit-your-teeth low.

And guess what? As much as it pains me to admit it, as bad a movie as *The Lost Boys* undoubtedly is (and sorry, kids, but it really is a bad movie), that's kind of all it is. It's not an abomination, or an abortion, or an abject failure of the medium. It's just a bad movie, that managed to get away with more success than it deserved in large part because of the elements that make it seem such a poor effort now—it's slavish devotion to everything that was current in the pop culture when it was made, or at least the most facile elements of that culture.

It's just an overrated, bad movie, nothing more, nothing less. The last time I watched it I was outraged by the disconnect between the film I remembered and the dross I was watching. This time?

This time I was just bored. And that's probably the healthiest reaction, honestly.

And should I ever want to revisit an actually good movie from the same period of my childhood... well, there's always RoboCop.

SHOW YOURSELF, DESTROY OUR FEARS, RELEASE YOUR MASK

Queen: Greatest Hits II

In Stephen King's *On Writing*, King makes a convincing case that writing is actually telepathy. He thinks something in his head, transcribes what he sees, and when you pick up the book and read it, blam, his thought is now in your head. He's serious about this, or at least claims to be, and the more I think about it, the more seriously I take it, too.

And I'm beginning to suspect that if writing is telepathy, maybe a musical recording is time travel.

It's Saturday 20th December 2014. I am Christmas shopping in The Centre:MK.

Pity me.

I'm shopping because, as usual, I've left it too late—let the calendar just run me over, every day an *I'll-do-it-tomorrow*, until it dawns that I'm out of tomorrows, and if I don't get it done, there's going to be some upset people in my immediate future.

So I join the hollow eyed hordes of Milton Keynes and surrounding environs, and engage with them in the mind numbing, soul crushing H-bomb ground zero of capitalistic spending that is the last shopping weekend before C-Day.

At some point, I make it to HMV, which is handy, as there are music CDs on my list. After some initial confusion, I work out that the CDs no longer occupy the huge ground floor as they used to (that's DVD/Blu Ray central now), but have instead been relegated to the much smaller upper deck. Trying not to feel a billion years old, I take the escalator, and browse. Sure enough, there's the CD I want to get. Even better, thanks to a special offer, I can save money by buying a second CD and spending more (yes, my mind works like this, no, I do not want to buy a bridge). I browse, finding only discs I already own or have no interest in buying. That is, until…

There it sits. Classic blue (navy? royal?), dark, the gold lettering, that coat of arms. I pick it up and read through the track listing, goosebumps running up my arms. I've never owned this, but I'm intimately familiar with it. I chuck it in the basket and buy it as part of the twofer offer, secure in the knowledge that no one will have got me it as a gift. How could they? I didn't even know I needed it until I saw it.

I get the rest of the shopping done, get in the car, but before I start the engine, before I even get my seatbelt on, I rummage in the HMV bag and pull out the CD. Again, I look at that cover. Read the words.

Queen: Greatest Hits II.

I'm smiling, but it's a small smile, a sad one. I feel it on my face.

I put the CD into the stereo and turn the key. Music plays.

It's probably the summer of 1992, so I will be fourteen years old. Freddie died the previous year, and the tribute concert blew my mind. And in my dad's small VHS collection, I find a video: *Queen: Greatest Flix II.*

The cover is deep, dark blue. The crest on the front looks amazing: gold lettering and scrollwork. I put the video in and play. This trip, and subsequent ones, I will do this a lot, watching and rewatching. And listening. Most of all, listening.

'It's A Kind Of Magic' comes first. The video has the rest of the band in tramp outfits, and Freddie is the magician, cartoon sparks flying from his fingertips, turning them into rock stars, producing cartoon female backing singers. He reverses the spell at the end of the video, each finger click making something disappear. Each beat taking the magic further away.

Like the ticking of a clock.

I read the short booklet that came with the video a lot, especially once I'd become super familiar with the videos, which is how I know that the reason the 'Under Pressure' video features neither Queen nor David Bowie is because they were both on tour, so instead stock footage is combined with clips from the black and white Nosferatu movie to follow the themes of the song. Initially, that put me off, and the song is marked as a fast forward track, but later, when I force myself to listen to all the songs, it will go back into the must listen category. Also, I'll get it

SHOW YOURSELF, DESTROY OUR FEARS...

straight in my head that Vanilla Ice stole this bass line from Queen and not the other way around, which helps.

In 2014, I sing along in the car. Or I try. The Bowie parts are barely manageable. The Freddie parts are impossible.

Back in 1992-3, 'Radio Ga Ga' is a must-watch. Flying cars, I think is what sold it. Also *Metropolis*. Also, I think I liked the song. I think I responded to the affection in the vocal. 'Radio, someone still loves you.' The guitar in the fade-out is lovely too. Even then, I was a sucker for a nice guitar line.

On 20th April, 1992, I will watch Paul Young lead every single person in Wembley Stadium into handclaps during this song. I will watch this from my bedroom in North Devon and marvel. It will be years later before I see Freddie, on that same stage, huge, indomitable in that yellow jacket, leading a younger sold out crowd in 1986 through the same clapping ritual. The last year Queen toured as a unit. I was eight. I wasn't there at the time, but I have been there many, many times since.

Back in Dad's house in 1992-3, 'I Want It All' was definitely a must-play. I loved everything about it—the attitude, the riff, the lyric, the video, with the football stadium lights (according to that helpful booklet) making the band glow. The guitar solo is fucking amazing too—sure, there's shitty synth hits running underneath (it was the 80s—nobody got out unscathed), but holy mother of God, Brian May can *play*. Great rundown at the end too.

Freddie looks thin, the suit and tie not hiding it. His cheeks are hollow. Killer vocals, though. In

2014, I again spectacularly fail to keep up with it; I'm glad my daughter is not in the car to hear her old man's voice crack up on the high notes.

Back in 1992-3 'I Want To Break Free' is another must-play. If you've seen the video, you know why. The band dressed in Coronation Street drag—Freddie resplendent in pink and black spandex, pushing a hoover around, magnificent Village People moustache in full view (at least until the ballet sequence, where it mysteriously vanishes; I think the booklet explained why, but I forget). Also in 1992 news, Roger Taylor makes a good enough looking woman that I am confused watching this the first few times, wondering who the hot blond is and what they've done with the drummer.

No, I do not want to buy a bridge.

And then…

It's Sunday 27th January, 1991. I am twelve. We are driving home from Exeter to the village I grew up in. It's dark. We listen to the top 40 on the radio. Actually, as we've tuned in around 6:15, we're more catching the top 15 or so. I will have heard Jesus Jones and Rick Astley, and I will not have cared. I will also have heard The Farm and Vanilla Ice, and probably did care a bit—that 'Ice, Ice, Baby' bass line was pretty sweet. 'The Bartman' was new in at number 11. Sky TV being a thing rich kids had, and me not being a rich kid, Bart was an icon of aspirational, untouchable cool. I had a flattop haircut and everything. *So* cool. The song would later be number one.

But not this week.

SHOW YOURSELF, DESTROY OUR FEARS...

The fucking 'Grease fucking Megamix', curse of wedding discos to this day, was clinging to the bottom of the top 10. Back then I probably enjoyed it, or at least didn't mind it. I did mind 'I've Had The Time Of My Life' though—passionately hated it, in fact. Seal was number 4 with 'Crazy'. He had a decent voice, but I wasn't wild about the song.

KLF at number 2.

Then they read out the whole top 40, making you wait for the big one. Blah, blah, blah, 4, Seal, 3, Enigma, 2, KLF…

'So it's a brand new single straight in at number one this week—Queen. *Innuendo*.'

'Ooh, I really like The Queen!' says mum, and cranks the radio.

A snare rolls.

'1… 2… 3… 4…!'

Synth strings fade-in, minor, menacing. The drumbeat is military. A guitar growls in the background, feeds back, then the drums swell, and Brian May shreds the world in two with an explosive chord that rings and rings, that amazing guitar tone singing, wailing.

It's hypnotic, disconcerting, epic. Scary. Freddie sings his heart out, a towering vocal performance from a master, full of passion but also longing, darkness, desperation. Fear.

The whole thing is disorienting, the riff jagged, the rhythm unusual, the vocal line fast and complex. Then, just as you have a handle on it, just as a recognisable, repeatable pattern has become apparent, a verse and chorus, something to wrap your mind around, everything drops away, and the song slows almost to a stop. Then a Spanish guitar, exquisitely played, hands clapping. (In 1992-3, the claymation Commedia dell'arte clowns will delight and unsettle me in equal measure as they dance around the screen and perform acrobatics. By then I'll be familiar enough with the song that I'll know all its twists and turns, and it will be like a beloved and oft-taken roller-coaster ride. But that's 1992. This is the first ride). It's incredible, haunting.

Then, just as you've adjusted to that, it changes again, more synth strings, swirling, as Freddie sings:

You can be anything you want to be,
Just turn yourself into anything you think that you could ever be,
Be free with your temple! Be free! Be free!
Surrender your ego! Be Free! Be Free! To yourself...

Then Brian May brings the thunder, Roger Taylor assisting with power and precision. The guitar explodes into a flurry of notes, playing the previous acoustic riff at breakneck pace, the familiar rendered strange by the full on distortion, before shrieking and peeling off into a blistering solo. The guitar sings, it wails, it growls. The hairs on the back of my twelve-year-old arm stand. I have no clue what is going on, but I know it's both unsettling and magnificent.

Six minutes and thirty seconds. That's how long it can take to change a life. I have no fucking idea what just happened, but I am awestruck.

My mum turns to me, grinning. 'Well, that was bloody brilliant! Wasn't it?'

I can't talk. So I nod instead.

It's Sunday 27th January, 1991, and Queen are number 1 with 'Innuendo', and all is right with the world.

Freddie Mercury has ten months to live.

Back in 2014, 'It's A Hard Life' starts playing. This was an always fast-forward track in 1992-3, and I get to the first chorus before tipping my hat to fourteen-year-old me and skipping. Can't win them all, I think. The goddamn 80s soiled everyone. Plus, how do you follow 'Innuendo'?

'Breakthru'! I'm back in 1992-3, watching that train burst through the polystyrene wall with the word 'NOW!' spray-painted on it. What a fucking great video. The band on the back of a steam train, rocking out. Hair blowing in the wind. Freddie (thin, yeah, but still vital, still looking like he's having fun) vamping and leaping about like the goddamn rock star he was. Is. Will always be. I remember hearing 'The Boys Of Summer' years later, and wondering why you'd rip off this chorus riff without resolving it properly. My mind knows better, but in my heart, I really believe this still.

Fuck chronology.

Then, oh shit, it's 'Who Wants To Live Forever'.

It's April 20th, 1992. I am watching the Freddie Mercury tribute concert on the black and white TV in my room. In my father's house in MK, the VHS is recording it, and in my bedroom in the ass end of North Devon, the cassette tape is getting everything from the broadcast on Radio 1. It's been a blast so far, a fucking party. Metallica and Guns N' Roses (and yeah, okay, Extreme) have all been on my TV, and everyone was watching! These are *my* fucking bands, and they're on TV in front of everyone! Holy fucking shit! I won't feel this way again until Christmas 2010, when in the week my daughter comes into the world, the Christmas number 1 is Rage Against The Machine. The feeling that the things I love, that I had accepted then, and now, were objects of ridicule and contempt, instead became moments of celebration and defiance.

Give me a second.

Okay.

The bands have come and gone, and now we have what Tommy Vance on Radio 1 has dubbed 'The Queen Superset!' and it is mind-blowingly awesome. Already, we've had 'Tie Your Mother Down' with Joey Elliot from Def Leppard, Roger fucking Daltrey singing 'I Want It All' (and cheating on the key, though I won't learn that until much later, when I discover that, unlike the Queen recording, I can actually sing along with this version without injuring myself), 'Hammer To Fall', fucking James fucking Hetfield singing 'Stone Cold Crazy', Robert Plant taking a swing at 'Innuendo', and the aforementioned Paul Young and 'Radio Ga Ga', and I'm buzzing my nuts off, in the parlance of our times, high as a kite on the music, the occasion...

(If none of that means anything to you—I'm sorry. I'm so, so sorry. There's still time. Educate yourself. Your life will be better for it. Trust me.)

And then, they announce Seal, and my heart just

sinks. I mean, sure, the cat can sing, but come on, man. You've got David Bowie and Axl Rose back there, and you're giving me Seal?

Bummer, dude. Not cool.

'I wanted to sing this song because I remember when I first heard it in a movie and it made me cry.'

Oh brother, I think.

Later, in a to-camera interview, he will say, 'I wanted to sing that song ["Who Wants To Live Forever"?] but then I tried it, and I was like, I can't do this, it'll end my career, man!'

Then he sings.

> *There's no time for us,*
> *There's no place for us*
> *What is this thing that fills our dreams*
> *Yet slips away from us?*

All of a sudden there's a lump in my throat. He's clearly nervous, terrified even, but he's doing it.

> *There's no chance for us,*
> *It's all decided for us…*

I think about Freddie. About a man who could sing like an opera star but chose rock 'n roll. I think about his flamboyance, his stage presence, his ability to take a stadium of people, tens of thousands, and hold them all in the palm of his hand.

> *This world has only one sweet moment,*
> *Set aside for us…*

I think about all the things he'll never get to do. The shows he'll never play. The ones I'll never see. I'll think about how no one will ever see Freddie sing 'Innuendo' live. It'll never happen, can't happen.

He's dead.

My chest starts to hurt. So do my eyes.

> *Who wants to live forever?*
> *Who wants to live forever?*

Seal cannot hit the next note. He knows it. You can hear it in his voice as it approaches. It's too much, and he doesn't have it in him.

And then he does it anyway.

The hairs on my fourteen-year-old arm stand, and I cry.

> *When love must die...*

It's June 1992. I've just turned fourteen, and my birthday present from my dad, by my request, is an Our Price voucher. I use the £20 voucher to buy three albums on cassette. One is *Southern Harmony and Musical Companion* by The Black Crowes. It got five stars in Raw magazine, and I'm curious. It will transform my life.

The second is Rage Against The Machine's debut. I'd wanted to own this album since I saw the band play 'Killing In The Name' on The Word the previous year, when my thirteen-year-old brain was scrambled by the carnage they wreaked on that show. The album will not disappoint. In fact, it will also change my life. The band I later become a part of in

2004 will pick 'Know Your Enemy' as a cover, and play it at our final show. The RATM set at Leeds festival in 2008 (immediately followed by Slipknot) will be one of the definitive live shows of my life. And as noted above, 'Killing In The Name' will, against all laws of sanity and market driven pop music, be the number one single the week my daughter is born.

Oh, sorry. The third cassette?

Queen, *Live At Wembley, '86*.

Freddie: 'There's been a lot of rumours going round, about a certain band called Queen... And the rumours are that we're going to split up. What do you think?'

The crowd roars.

'They're talking from here!'

The crowd laughs.

'I must tell you, I keep wanting to leave but they won't let me! Also...'

He lets the laugh crest for a second before continuing. Ever the crowd pleaser.

'...Also, I suppose, we're not bad for four aging queens, really, are we?'

The crowd cheers.

'So forget those rumours, we'll stay together 'till we fucking well die, I'm sure of it.'

The crowd roars again. It is 1986. Freddie has already been diagnosed with HIV, though he has told no one. He knows there's every chance this is the last tour.

'This one is a new song, it's called "Who Wants To Live Forever"...'

It's 1986, and Freddie knocks it clear out of

Wembley Stadium. It's 1992, and Seal does the same. It's impossible, but he does it away. And I weep. In joy and sadness. In celebration and despair. Mortality is suddenly too close. If it can take a man like Freddie, a god like that, strike him down in the prime of his life, fuck. Nobody is safe. None of us.

Also, he's gone. That too is impossible, and true.

It's 2014. I've driven the long way home, gone around at least two excessive roundabouts, but still I'm home, and the record is still playing. Somehow I don't crash, even though I can barely see for the tears in my eyes when... 'Forever' comes on. So I park on the drive, and leave the CD playing, 'Headlong' is next.

In 1992-3, this too is an always play. The riff is a dirty rocker, that's all. The video is fun too, just the guys goofing off in the studio. Freddie is thin again, but he looks like he's having fun. They all do.

> *And you're rushing Headlong,*
> *Out of control,*
> *And you think you're so strong,*
> *But there ain't no stoppin',*
> *And there's nothin' you can do about it...*

'The Miracle' was also a must play. My cousin said she knew the kid who played John Deacon in the video. More fundamentally, it's children getting to be Queen in a Queen video. As a child myself, it was hypnotising. The fantasy made flesh. Apparently, the kid was a bit of an asshole in real life. This information did little to burst my bubble. In 2014,

SHOW YOURSELF, DESTROY OUR FEARS...

I'm less impressed—the production is horrible, so 80s, and the song feels trite; sentimental in a bad way—a precursor to the disappointments of 'Made In Heaven'. But in 1992-3, I watched and listened and enjoyed it every time. Especially the look on Brian May's face when kid Brian May bogarts his second guitar solo. There's a genuinely musically weird part at the end too, when that solo is still playing and the coda bleeds over the top, creating a discordant noise that is at once hypnotic and unsettling:

> *That time will come,*
> *One day you'll see,*
> *When we can all be friends...*

Next video (must-watch, of course) is 'I'm Going Slightly Mad'. This is the penultimate that Freddie shot (the last being 'These Are The Days Of Our Lives', put out after his death and not part of this collection), but the booklet in 1992-3 makes no mention of this, it having been written before Freddie's illness was made public. I loved the black and white. The mad wig. The visuals that followed the lyric—Freddie with a hat of bananas, John Deacon's kettle helmet. The bass run at the end, with John Deacon fast-running up a staircase before disappearing, leaving only his jesters hat floating in mid-air? Genius.

It's sometime between Christmas and New Year, 2014. I'm in the car with my daughter (born in the year of Rage Against The Machine, 2010, world without end, amen), who is soon to be five, and the CD is still in the stereo and playing, and 'The Invisible Man' comes on. At the end of the first chorus, my little girl is singing along, and I look over my shoulder and see she is dancing in her car seat, grinning.

Achievement unlocked.

In 1992-3, it's an always play, because the video is based on a computer game, or an idea of what computer games are, and I'm a nerd, so yeah.

'Hammer To Fall'. Funny story with the video for this one. They shot it at a concert, and Queen asked the audience to come back the next day to complete the video shoot for the song, and according to the booklet, only fourteen people turned up for the shoot. I remember at fourteen years old thinking how pathetic that was, and how dumb those no-shows must now feel, realising what they missed.

Promising myself I would never be That Guy.

What the hell we fighting for?
Just surrender and it won't hurt at all,
Just got time to say your prayers,
Then it's time for the hammer to fall...

'Friends Will Be Friends' was an always play too. What can I say? I was a sentimental child. These days, it takes me a bottle of wine or a quarter bottle of whiskey to connect with feelings that then were at the surface. The video was lovely, too—members of the Queen fan club getting, in effect, a command performance, even if of only one song. Freddie still looks good too—they played a verse of this as part of the Wembley '86 encore medley, so when the video was shot, everything still looked good. No sign of the problems that would so soon come to dominate.

Then it's 'The Show Must Go On'. Another 92-93 must-play, and it had to be for the song rather than the video. The reason I say that is because, by the time the video was produced, Freddie was too ill to film, so it had to be put together via clips of all the other videos I had already seen on the tape, which, irony, huh, considering the title?

But what a goddamn song.

> *Inside my heart is aching,*
> *My makeup may be flaking*
> *But my smile still stays on...*

Montage. Freddie in the 'Breakthru' video, dancing with a girl. In black and white, with the bananas...

I guess I'm learning, I must be stronger now,
I'll soon be turning, round the corner now...
I mean, come on.

> *I'll face it with a grin,*
> *I'm never giving in,*
> *On with the show...*

Brian May solos as the set of Highlander explodes behind him...

> *I've topped the bill,*
> *I love the kill,*
> *I have to find the will to carry on...*

MY LIFE IN HORROR VOLUME I

Freddie wails from the 'I Want It All' video...

Show must go on...

But it can't. It's almost over.
There's one song left.

It's 12th July 1986. Wembley Stadium. Following their barnstorming performance at Live Aid the previous year, and the release of the *A Kind Of Magic* album, Queen have bounced back from an obscurity threatening disco album (*Hot Space*) to being the hottest live ticket London has seen. Queen is filming the gig to produce a concert home video. The night before, rain caused problems with the filming, but on this day, the sun is shining on the capacity crowd. INXS opened, The Alarm and Status Quo have been and gone, and now the crowd awaits the main event. The band they've paid £14.50 to see.

A distorted vocal washes over the crowd, quickly joined by strings, and the audience cheers. They know. As the intro tape plays over the speakers, the band backstage warm up. Brian May checks his shoulder strap, and is satisfied. John Deacon looks, as ever, supernaturally calm, composed (favourite drink: Tea, according to the *Killer Queen* video). And Freddie, resplendent in the yellow jacket, flexes his legs on the ramp up to the stage, taut and ready.

The crowd clap, faster and faster, their rhythm impatient. They've paid. They want to see the show. The strings build and build. Smoke fills the stage. The crowd roars in anticipation. Then Freddie and Brian burst from the smoke, Freddie almost sprinting

SHOW YOURSELF, DESTROY OUR FEARS...

to meet the audience. The roar explodes, reverberates around the stadium. Freddie holds his half mic stand aloft in his fist, smiling. Transcendent. Immortal. A man at the peak of his considerable powers. A man in his element, doing what he was born to do. What he lives to do. We love him. He loves us.

All is right with the world.

The intro tape strings crescendo. Brian May hits a riff that splits the sky in two.

Queen rock out. The audience loses their minds.

One man, one goal, Ha, one mission...

IT'S JUST A PHASE I WAS GOING THROUGH

The Wasp Factory

Thirteen or fourteen—I can be no more precise. Dad had—has still, if I know my old man—a collection of the non-M paperbacks. Beautiful black covers with white artwork and words. That he had a whole set, eight or ten titles at that point, clearly boded well—my dad reads a ton, but he's not what Mr. King refers to as much of a constant reader—he likes finding new things, new stories, new writing. Very rare that my dad will buy everything someone puts out. I also remember this being one of the few books I borrowed from my dad that was a real loan, and not a 'borrow' that ended up living with me on a more permanent basis. He explicitly asked for the book back when I was done. That was another sign, looking back.

How had the name come to my attention? Playground gossip? It's vanishingly unlikely, given where I went to school and my peer group, but it feels like that was the source. I have a strong sense that I was aware of the book prior to seeing it on my father's shelf, that it held some legendary status of twisted, fucked up writing far worse than the King or Koontz or Herbert catalogue I'd been exposed to. I

IT'S JUST A PHASE I WAS GOING THROUGH

approached the book with trepidation, is what I'm trying to say, and I think that came from outside. Though Dad will probably have let me know, casually, that it was dark, or scary.

Many of you will have heard such hype as a kid, about a book or movie. I think one of the principle experiences of growing up is the first time you sit and watch or read something that has been hyped and are underwhelmed. It's a rite of passage—the moment you first look at a piece of art (defined broadly) for which someone else has professed love, admiration or fear, and asked, 'is this it?' I'm unsure I can pinpoint when that first happened for me.

This sure as shit was not that day.

Because *The Wasp Factory* by Iain Banks did not merely live up to the hype, it exceeded it in every way. It transcended it. It blew the fucking doors off.

And listen: this whole book carries a gigantic spoiler warning, but I'm going to double down on that now: if you're a fan of horror or dark fiction—any kind of fan at all of this genre—and you haven't yet read this book, you need to stop reading right fucking now, go away and get it, and read it, and then come back. I am not kidding. I am going to talk about this book in detail, and… look, it's like *Fight Club*, or *The Sting*, or *The Sixth Sense*, or *The Crying Game*. Nothing can recreate that first time you experience the story, get to *that* moment, and go 'holy fucking *Hell*!' *The Wasp Factory* is that good. Maybe better. And I don't want to be responsible for spoiling it for anyone. So sincerely, go and read this goddamn book. Thank me later.

The book is terrifying. It grossed me out on a

visceral level, at points, but more importantly, it went after me where I lived. The protagonist is deranged. As the story winds out, you discover how deranged, but even from early on, it's clear he's messed up. There's something sinister about having a story told to you by a young man who is clearly bright, articulate, intelligent, and deeply horrible. None of this 'save the cat' bullshit here—Frank is unpleasant from the get-go, and by the third or fourth chapter, it's clear he's an outright monster. I remember a clammy, claustrophobic feeling to reading the book—like being trapped in a bar with a drunk man you gradually realise is also unhinged and dangerous, who has decided that you are to be his audience for the evening. You are afraid of him, and what he will tell you... but you are also too scared to walk away (as we'll discuss in *Volume II*, I speak from personal experience).

But/and/also... he's a teenage boy, with views that will not be completely alien to anyone who was also a teenage boy in the early 90s, especially if that someone (okay, yes, you've cracked the code, me) was bought up in a rural environment. The casual misogyny, sure, but also, let's be really honest, some of the magical thinking, too; the notion that one *is* kind of the centre of the universe; that the events that surround one have a significance, are in part a response to, and in part a message for, *you.*

It's a powerful memory—that sense of dread and mirror-darkly recognition that propelled me through the story. It's a lesson that's stuck with me as a writer—all that stuff about having to have a sympathetic protagonist—well, here's a debut novel from a young to-that-point sci-fi writer that deliberately, almost surgically, cuts against that premise, presenting instead a character who only becomes more frightening the more layers you peel away, and compels your attention by, in effect, daring you to look away.

I couldn't. I couldn't as he discussed his divination device—The Wasp Factory—a device that he feeds wasps into, which contains a series of death traps for the creatures, and by which death he seeks to understand the future and how he should act. I couldn't as he calmly described the childhood accident that robbed him of his genitals—a savage dog attack. I couldn't as he calmly talked about his brother, recently escaped from an insane asylum, on his way back to the remote Scottish island Frank lives on with his father.

I couldn't as he calmly tells us of the murders Frank committed as a child.

He describes the murders of two other children. The first I have no memory of, beyond the fact of it, though I feel afraid just trying to remember. The second, though, haunts me to this day, primarily because of its clinical cruelty. Simply put, he contrives to tie a young girl (seven? eight? no older) to a giant kite, and simply sails it off a cliff and out over the sea. While she is fully awake and aware. To float until she lands in the sea, there to sink and drown—or, perhaps, carried high enough to die from exposure, I guess. The story is told from Frank's perspective, so we never learn the specifics of her ending (Frank himself couldn't care less, only glad to be rid of the annoyance, and if I recall the body is never found), and we are left instead to imagine the horror of her predicament, as she is carried beyond all possible safety, into a cold, terrifying and painful death.

And there is worse. Far worse. Frank's brother has a nasty habit, you see; it is a habit of trying to force younger children to eat worms. This is the behaviour that finally lands him in the institution from which he escapes at the start of the book. As the book evolves, we find out the cause of this derangement. It's one of the most horrific passages of prose I can recall, and even at this distance of twenty years, I reel in fear, disgust… and worst of all, a bleak darkness, a feeling that there is something fundamentally wrong with the world, something broken and diseased at its centre. It's an acknowledgement that there are things that can happen that are so awful, not only can there not be a loving God, but there may in fact only be his dark mirror; some bleak, vicious jester. Not simply because of some particular piece of gross out imagery—though that is part of it, and a spectacularly imaginative image too—but rather because of the notion of blissful unawareness, even pleasure, that accompanies said image. This does not merely gross out the stomach—it grosses out the mind.

And yes, it's a work of fiction, something Iain Banks made up. But you know that thing about how good fiction is a lie told in service to the truth? Well, this is one of those. I've thought about this a lot, because I'm conscious that if you haven't read the book (and seriously, if that's you and you've got this far, I love you, but *fuck off* and read it, okay?) you may not get what I got—my reaction may not be yours. You may have read enough other heinous shit that it doesn't resonate in the same way, or your mind may just not have the same triggers mine does. In other words, I am acutely aware that I may be, in point of fact, setting you up for the kind of disappointment I talked about up top.

Well okay. And if that is the case for you, I apologise. But I have to say for me, this book redefined what horror could be. With not a single ghost, monster, killer clown, vampire or satanic ritual, it disturbed me more than any work of fiction had to that point. And honestly, casting my mind over what I've read since, with the possible exception of *Sleepers* (which cheats by being based on a true story) and *Exquisite Corpse*, I think it still holds that crown.

And I just can't do it. I can't bring myself to write the spoiler filled discussion I usually would. For two reasons. One, I know damn well that somebody ignored my last two warnings and is still gleefully reading in ignorance of the text—and fuck you, go and read the fucking book. But far more importantly, two, I can't do it justice. Taken from context, quoted out of a twenty-year memory rather than expressed word for word, as part of the surrounding story, it just won't have the pile-driving, life changing impact on you that it had on me. If you've read it, you know what it is I'm talking about. If you haven't, well, did I mention fuck you? But also, I can't do it justice.

I am not as good a writer as Iain Banks. And it's a near certainty that you aren't either.

Banks was a singular talent. *The Wasp Factory* is

one of the greatest horror novels of the 80s. In fact, I'd argue it's one of the greatest horror novels written full stop. Proof positive that you don't need to have monsters to write heart-stopping, gut churning horror. Proof positive that you can rip up the rule book about likeable, sympathetic, relatable narrators, as long as you're capable of writing prose so fucking compelling people are too scared to look away. Living, seething proof that horror doesn't need to be dumb, or lowest common denominator, or any of that shit that gets flung at it; more, proof that the best horror is amongst the best writing in print, no qualifier needed—fierce, whip smart, unflinching, gripping, compelling, and sure, terrifying.

Banks went on to write a lot of what was called 'literary fiction' between his sci-fi novels, and some of them I'd similarly label as non-supernatural horror (*A Song Of Stone* being a particularly bleak and fine example). The fact that we don't talk about *The Wasp Factory* as a great horror novel is entirely a failure of us as a genre—a lack of confidence, maybe, or just a too-blind acceptance of the categories we're given by publishers scared of being labelled as horror. If Cormac McCarthy is horror (and he fucking is) then so is Iain Banks—or at least, *The Wasp Factory* is. In fact, I'll say it again—*The Wasp Factory* is one of the greatest horror novels of the Twentieth Century.

Look, I'll do you a deal; go read this book if you haven't already. Then we'll talk, okay? We can talk about all those lovely twists, that heart stopping reason behind Frank's brother's illness, the truth regarding Frank's father, the murders, all of it. I want to, believe me. This book did some damage to my mind, frankly—showed me the limits of what I thought fiction could do, could talk about, and could effect, were entirely a failure of my imagination—that, in point of fact, fiction could open your eyes to not just darker realities, but darker corners of this actual, shared reality—the world we live and breathe in. It is a monumental, monstrous, marvellous book, and it may change your life.

Go read it. Then we'll talk.

WE HAVE SUCH SIGHTS TO SHOW YOU

Hellraiser

Unpacking this one is tough, with any moral certainty. Here's the problem—I watched *Hellraiser II* first. I had not, prior to that point, seen a huge amount of movie horror of the eighteen-certificate variety, and as you might expect… it had an impact. Not to take away from *Hellraiser*, which is by any measure an impressive achievement, but I saw it later, and after *II*, and that changed things. One symptom of that is this inability to clearly state the time and location I first saw *Hellraiser*.

I'm going to have to guess.

And my guess is my fifteenth birthday.

That year, we had a VCR. That year, I decided what I wanted was for Bev to stay over and sleep on the sofa so we could stay up all night watching horror movies. Mum, perhaps infected by Video Van Man disease, agreed, and allowed us to pick any movies from the 'local' store (actually seven miles away, but that's rural life). I remember I optimistically rented eight movies, figuring at two hours each that would get us to dawn—maths clearly not a strong suit even then. Surprisingly, we didn't manage to watch all the films. To the best of my recollection, the films we rented were:

Aliens
Return Of The Living Dead
Evil Dead
Evil Dead 2
Army Of Darkness—Medieval Dead
Hellraiser
Hellraiser 2

And some other film that was fifteen-certificate—possibly *The Lost Boys*, though I can't say for sure.

And my memory is that we'd saved the Hellraiser films for the finale. So it will have been with bleary eyes and a numb mind that I first encountered the full story of Frank Cotton and Julia, poor Larry and the spectacularly unfortunate Kirsty.

It was riveting.

The opening sequence grabbed me by the scruff of the neck. There's a lovely moment as Frank gets up to leave, having bought the puzzle box, and pauses, like he's expecting the salesman to make some smart-assed remark, then he goes... then the salesman does, indeed, make a smart-assed remark. It's intentionally funny, which makes the opening of the box moments later, with all the hooks-into-bleeding-flesh gory detail, all the more shocking.

There's an incredible elegance to the story-telling too—for all that we get Frank's voice-over exposition for anyone who came in five minutes late, in the opening sequence it's all told with, I think, no words. The box opens, out come the hooks, Frank is reduced to bloody parts, then Pinhead closes the puzzlebox, and they all disappear, leaving the room empty.

And then, Larry and Julia let themselves in.

Again, the storytelling is visual, mainly—we learn of Frank's previous presence in the house, and his relationship to Larry, very quickly. The reveal that Julia had a torrid affair with the bad-boy brother is revealed through a flashback. There's an incredible sequence where she's fantasising about their rutting, the grunting of their remembered union echoed by the grunts of her husband and the workmen trying to get the mattress up the stairs, the protruding nail in focus long before the pushing shoves Larry's hand into it, Larry's blood hitting the ground, and that blood draining into the floor as soon as Larry and Julia leave, resulting in the rebirth of Frank...

And I'll let you know when I go back for the rewatch, but my memory is that the effects were insanely impressive here, and in general around Frank, as he's slowly restored to life, flesh returning to bones fitfully, painfully.

As I write, I'm discovering I have a very good recall of this film, better than I suspected when I sat down. I imagine that's because I owned the Cinema Club edition on VHS at a later date, and clearly rewatched it a number of times. But I also think that it's inherently memorable cinema. By fifteen I will have seen the *Elm Streets*, *Terminator*, *Aliens*, and sundry *Hammer Horrors*. This one feels special. Sure, there's an iconic 'villain' and yes, he gets all the best lines ('No tears, please. It's a waste of good suffering.'), and sure, we've got the young woman heroine, so far, so 80s horror, but...

I think it's the mythos. The puzzle box itself appears semi-sentient, malevolent, and when it's 'solved' to release the Cenobites, it looks evil.

The Cenobites themselves are superb creations, mercifully from an age when the physical effect was still king. They look real as hell, and scary. And then in the middle of all this, a twisted 'love' story about destructive sexual desire, with a Lady Macbeth performance for the ages.

I know I made it to the end. I also know I fell asleep before *Hellbound* had finished (ask me about those dreams sometime…), so it's fair to say I will have been feeling pretty pummelled. But there was zero doubt I'd seen something special. Did I know how special? Maybe not. I feel like… and this may well just be bullshit old man nostalgia—almost has to be—but I feel like I was really lucky to come up when I did. I feel like in terms of horror cinema, I happened to be the right age to catch a string of classic movies that stand the test of time and have been rarely equalled since. I feel like I came up in a kind of golden age for the genre, and maybe the one sad thing about that is that I didn't appreciate how special some of what I was watching was. It's only now, when I can look back at what's been made subsequently, that I can appreciate the sheer raw tonnage of inventiveness, skill and talent poured into these films. *Hellraiser* is gross-out gore in places, for sure, and as noted, the tent poles of the genre are firmly in place. But bloody hell there's some incredible intelligence in the cinematic storytelling, an understanding and love of film, note perfect performances, and it all comes together in this sublimely paced 90 minute package. *Hellraiser* is one of the greats, and was probably wasted on fifteen-year-old me.

Fuck it—let's see, shall we?

Later

Yes, yes, yes. Recall is good. I was right about the elegance of the storytelling, for one. That continues throughout the movie, keeping things to a tight and taut 90 minutes. The performances are great too—the leads, of course, but even the supporting cast. Kirsty's love interest is a little two-dimensional, but the dinner guests are fantastic. Even better are Julia's three victims, each a brilliantly sketched model of lonely desperation, masked to a greater or lesser degree. The second is my personal favourite—in just two lines, I know him well enough to not be remotely sad when Julia bashes his brains in only thirty seconds later. That's skilled writing, folks.

And the makeup! Yes, the special effects—and one thing I had forgotten at a conscious level is how good the sound is for Frank's regeneration and in general, clanking chains on wood, oozing, slurping draining, ah, so, so visceral and brilliantly yucky—but the actual makeup transformation of Julia from slightly cold and aloof wife to near deranged with terror through to ice maiden is a goddamn triumph. Clare Higgins is a national treasure, and her performance here is equally compelling and terrifying, but the use of different makeup to highlight the changes in her internal psychological landscape is apt storytelling few will notice but most will feel. The paleness of her skin as she tries to clean the blood off her face after killing her first victim, coupled with the haunted look she gives the mirror (us) through smudged eyeliner—chilling. Contrast that with her later poise once she has hit her murdering stride, and the way she sets herself up for subsequent seductions, and we have no less than a masterclass in visual storytelling.

Then we have Frank. And just, I don't have the words. The three stages of Frank are surely taught in horror makeup master-classes to this day, right? Sure, they fuck about with the lighting for the first incarnation, and that may have been a necessity rather than a virtue for all I know, but as we learned from Jaws, it scarcely matters—the impact is what counts, and boy are we impacted. And once he gets his nerve endings back and starts smoking again—wow. I love the way there's ooze dripping from him in every shot, how he gleams with… whatever he's gleaming with. And that voice, emanating from that grotesque frame… So spooky. The love affair works too—probably because of the voice, I mean, it's Frank, right? We know it—so does Julia. It should be a gross out moment for the ages, yet somehow becomes almost touching, in a profoundly disturbing way.

Which brings us neatly to Pinhead and the Cenobites. One thing I had completely misremembered is how little the film features some of the most iconic creations in horror cinema (or, for my money, cinema full stop). Thanks to whoever made the decision to feature Pinhead front and centre on every poster and piece of publicity, we know what is coming, what we are to face. It's an image that inspires dread, revulsion. Yet, with the exception of a brief glimpse in the introduction, the main man is entirely absent from his movie until the half hour mark. Even then, he's only present as a further flashback, a mute figure observing Frank's suffering with cold detachment alongside his grotesque companions. They don't speak until well past the hour mark, and the impact when they do is profound.

Because it's at that moment, as Kirsty opens the box in the hospital, that we feel the deepest horror. Thanks to the flashbacks, we know what these creatures are capable of, and when The Chatterer shoves his fingers in Kirsty's mouth and Pinhead recites the mantra of the box ('You opened it. We came.') in that rich baritone, so full of controlled menace and authority, it really is a bowel loosener for the ages. Ashley Lawrence as Kirsty sells the hell out of this scene, mind-melting terror giving a manic desperation to her thinking. You can almost see the hamster wheels spinning as she desperately reaches for a way out, as she connects the horror of her confrontation with Frank to the box and the Cenobites, the intuitive leap fuelled by soul-deep horror. It's a wonderful moment, played to perfection by all involved.

Also... well, here's the thing. There's a pleasing... simplicity to the moral code of Pinhead and his compatriots. They *do* have a kind of morality, or at least rules, and they follow them. I mean, you would not like to meet them in any kind of alley even in broad daylight, but...

But by this point in the movie, we've met at least one scarier monster—Frank. I mean, you could make a case for Julia too (and the sequel will put the matter gloriously beyond doubt), but at this point, it's clear that Frank is even worse, morally, than Julia—utterly amoral, motivated purely by self-interest and a lust indistinguishable from greed. Any lingering doubts on that score are removed when his skinless form makes a none-too-subtle attempt to rape his brother's daughter. That's about as gross as it gets, really. So by this point, once Kirsty has named Frank... we kind of like Pinhead, don't we? We want him to find Frank, and drag him kicking and screaming back to where he came from—it feels like justice. Frank is irredeemably evil. He deserves Hell. And so, we find ourselves allied with one of the darkest creations in the horror genre. Hell, by the time we're back at the house of the killers, and Frank-in-his-brother's-skin is telling Kirsty that everything is all right, we're practically yelling at the screen for Pinhead to come back and shred his lying, father-murdering ass.

Really, contemplate that for a second. Because let's face facts: there's something a little bit unsettling about our collective love affair with the horror movie villains of the 80s. Jason, Freddie, Michael, Leatherface... they're all really fucking horrible people, right? Even in the best-case scenario of Jason... Well, he's killed a ton of people over his mommy issues, and with what I'd call increasingly wafer-thin justification. The others are out-and-out psychotics, with Freddy the worst of the lot—child killer turned immortal dream murderer of the kids of the people who burned him? That's a pretty massive yuck.

And yet we loved them anyway, did we not? Sure we did. We were dumb teenagers, and we loved the movies so much, we grew to love the psychopaths that stalked through them, leaving an increasingly dismembered trail of carnage behind them. *Scream* did for me a pretty decent job of deconstructing that phenomenon, but I'd be lying if I didn't say it's something that occasionally bothered me. Bothers me. I mean, not enough to stop watching or anything, but still…

But here comes *Hellraiser*. And suddenly, we've got a villain, a monster, and yet one we really *can* root for. Not because he fails to be scary—Pinhead and the gang are about as bad as it's possible to be, unrepentant sadists who will commit you to an eternity of vile torments, violence and unending agony. No, we root for them because we've found someone who we think deserves that fate, and we want him to go, and Kirsty to be safe. The moment when Frank admits his crime and the lights turn blue, filtering through the boards of wood in the wall, our hearts rise even as our stomachs sink. Because Hell is coming for Frank, and that's both awesome and terrible.

And really, what finer tribute can there be to this extraordinary movie? It's the genius of Clive Barker's towering imagination that he can conceive of so unremittingly dark and terrifying a creation as Pinhead and the Cenobites, and then find a way to make us root for them, without once compromising or mitigating their awful nature. In this respect, it does tower over so many of the other movies of the period that I discuss here and in *Volume II*. I'll be looking out for it, but I doubt there will be a moment as simultaneously triumphant and terrifying as when Pinhead shouts 'This isn't for your eyes!'

No shit, man.

Sure, the denouement following that moment is

necessarily slightly anti-climactic, and I could have done without the scrap with the gate-guardian thing, and it's a little unfortunate that the loop ending ('What's your pleasure, sir?') needed walking back for the sequel, but these are pretty tiny quibbles in the face of such a colossal achievement.

Hellraiser is, simply put, one of the finest horror movies ever made. I loved it then, and love it now, and it is utterly worthy of that love.

LEFTOVERS TO BE

Parents

The phrase 'cult classic' is overused. It's often applied to mainstream successes, purely because they are a bit odd. For example, I find labelling anything David Lynch has been involved in from *Twin Peaks* on as 'cult' just... well, wrong. I like David Lynch's work, a lot, as it happens. But cult? Dude's a mainstream success, albeit one who has managed to do that without compromising his artistic vision. Which is utterly awesome, and all respect and praise due.

But it's not cult.

Cult needs to be small. Obscure. Flawed. If everyone on your friends list has heard of it, it's not cult. It's just a cool thing you like.

And basically, I'm not a cult guy. My ear isn't to the ground enough for that—I'm too busy failing to skim off the cream of mainstream offerings, in any popular culture genre, to have a realistic chance of finding some deserving second or third tier band, movie or TV show to enjoy. By the time I come across something, it's generally, by the definition given above, no longer cult—it's broken out, reached critical mass, if you can dig it. It may have been 'cult', but by the time I find it, chances are good it's graduated simply to 'classic'. And that was basically always true; inevitable, even, given the cultural backwater I grew up in. Not that people didn't try, and often with great and noble effort (see *Volume II* for more), but the weight of geography and cultural attitudes made it functionally impossible for me to find anything that could fairly be called a 'hidden gem'.

Except… there is *Parents*.

Parents was released in 1989. It was made for $3 million, and grossed $870,500 box office. It got a brief US DVD release, and so far none at all in the UK. It stars Randy Quaid, in his best screen performance, and probably no one else you've heard of. And by sheer fluke I saw it on TV in the UK as a teenager, as part of a horror movie season on one of the broadcast networks—BBC2 or Channel 4. Almost certainly it was part of one of my many Friday night efforts to stay up late to catch *Raw Power*.

Now, *Parents* is undeniably goofy. It's set in the 50s, in whitebread suburbia, and that's an inherently goofy setting. Randy Quaid, is, well, Randy Quaid, and though he exhibits a restraint in this film that becomes actively creepy, there's still an essentially goofy quality to, well, him. But the brilliance of *Parents* lies in how it recognises a great but underexplored aesthetic truth—goofy is only a very thin sliver away from creepy.

I mean, think about it for a second and it makes sense. Grotesque is what happens when you twist caricature up just another half inch. Turn the volume up to eleven on an old cartoon and the distorted sound will become harsh, grating. Tragedy is when I stub my toe; comedy is when you fall down a manhole and die.

231

That said, I'm struggling to think of a movie that gets and exploits this better than *Parents*.

It starts with Quaid, for me. That 50s buzz cut, the serious glasses, and his early, misplaced humour with his son. It's a brilliant performance, by turns utterly buttoned down, the kind of icy calm that makes you instinctively nervous, through to behaviour so exaggerated past comedy it turns into creepy, without ever landing on normal-functioning-human. When we look back on the culture and advertising of the 50s, there's an inherent eerie, pod person aspect to it, especially when it comes to the rigid enforcement of gender norms, and totalitarian representation of the nuclear family as the irreducible final form of society, of humanity. *Parents* nails that vibe, creating a suburban environment where every smile looks like an upside down scream, where the perpetual sheen of sweat on Dennis Quaid's forehead gives the lie to his preternaturally calm voice—and yes, where the increasing insistence of child Michael's parents that he eat up the unidentified meat they serve for dinner takes on an almost screamingly sinister tone, even as the actual words and actions could as easily be those of exasperated parents as… well… as what, exactly?

It's unclear, and it remains unclear for most of the film's 81 minute running time. It's the internet age, so you can look it up, but I'm not going to spoil it here, and my firm advice is that you shouldn't either, if by the end of this you decide to give the film a spin (and really, you should). One of the reasons this movie deserves more attention and love than it gets is precisely the way in which it spins out the central tension of what, exactly, the hell is going on in this family, well past the point where most movies would have come down on one side or the other.

A lot of that ambiguity is possibly because of the kid. Michael, played by Bryan Madorsky, who is about as far from a Hollywood leading child actor as you could have found in '89 (though he wouldn't have been out of place as one of the gang in *Stranger Things*). He's a quiet, shy, pale, awkward kid, with a vivid imagination that leads to some fairly spectacular nightmares. These sequences are beautifully shot, and yeah, they are a lot less impressive post *The Shining*, but that doesn't mean they aren't still effective. Steal from the best, and all that.

Beyond the very good, and occasionally actually brilliant direction, the kid turns in a superb performance. Mirroring the wider ambiguity of what the hell is (or is not) going on with his parents, Michael is straddling that line between quiet and withdrawn, imaginative and disturbed (if that is a line, and not just positive and negative spins on the same phenomenon). He's certainly a misfit, which in the hyper conformist atmosphere of the 50s setting places the viewer in constant anxiety for his wellbeing. This is amplified by intentionally showing us a sequence where his parent's behavior is understandable to the viewer but incomprehensible to him, further fuelling his imagination and nightmares, and for the audience heightening our anxiety as to what the truth of his situation might be.

The other strength, for me, is the movie doesn't cop out. It plays out the tension as long as it can—

indeed, far further than most movies would dare—but ultimately, the ambiguity is utterly dissolved, leading to a final fifteen minutes of high stress horror. Again, the cast performances in this sequence are brilliant, as are many of the directorial decisions—the film didn't have a massive budget, but some imaginative choices with camera positioning and movement help elevate some of the closing scenes.

In summary, *Parents* is a movie long overdue a critical reappraisal—it's a smartly made, well acted, quirky horror movie, and one where most of the horror is based in psychological tension, generated by the potential gap between the kid's perception of the world and reality. It's not perfect, and it's certainly not a gore fest, but if you're a fan of 80s horror, and this one passed you by, you could do a lot worse than treating yourself by hunting it down and checking it out.

If for no other reason than it unambiguously qualifies for the title 'cult classic'. And it's probably the only one I'll ever be able to recommend.

YOU LOOK LIKE A CLOWN IN THAT STUPID JACKET

Wild at Heart

No safety net this time. No Googling, no rewatches. This one's a free-fall with memory and scotch. Let's see where we land.

I'm going with '94, '95 tops. So I'm fifteen to sixteen. My memory is of Channel 4's 'Without Walls' season, but who the hell knows so far out? I've got a feeling—and this applies to a lot of what I've written about, though I haven't yet mentioned it—that when I first recorded it from the telly, I may have missed the opening. Or maybe on the first viewing I arrived ten minutes in. That feels significant. Like an artefact of the analogue world we've all but left behind. How often will my daughter have to endure the indignity of watching a movie from the fifteen-minute marker? Never, is my guess, unless by choice, what with OD and iPlayer and +1 and Netflix and YouTube and all the rest. Digital means never having to say, 'Oh well, I missed the beginning.'

Doesn't matter. I went back and watched the whole thing many, many times. Last viewing was several years ago, with the missus. She didn't like it much. Which is a valid response. It's one of those films.

Me, I love it.

First, it's about fire, burning. Lots of close ups on matches, smouldering cigarettes. Amorphous flaming backgrounds over the titles. Beautiful, roaring, yellow, orange, red. And of course a fire forms a significant moment in the film—there's an argument to be made that the reveal of the events of a fire is the pivot moment of the movie, the moment when it turns from a slightly surreal but fun road trip picture into something altogether darker, weirder, and scarier.

But I'm getting ahead of myself.

We open, if memory serves, in Cape Fear. There's a year given, but it eludes me. Glen Miller's 'In The Mood' is playing (the first time I typed that it came out Frank Miller, which I think I would pay to hear, but alas). Gorgeous ballroom ceiling. A young Laura Dern is wearing a dress. She is also gorgeous. A young-ish-but-older-than-her black man says, 'Yo Sailor, wait up!' Then he takes her hand and in a quieter voice says, 'You're mine, baby.' Her face indicates intense dislike at this sentiment.

The man catches up with Nick Cage, who is also young and also gorgeous. Additionally, he wears a jacket of some distinction.

'You know, I been talking to Tallulah's momma.'

'Uh-oh!' Nick is breathing heavy, sweating. He is grinning but his teeth are clenched. He looks crazy scared or crazy angry. Maybe both.

'She said you been trying to fuck her in the toilet for the last ten minutes!' He laughs at this. Maybe this is where Mr. Cage says, 'Uh-oh.'

'You're one sick puppy! Tryin' to fuck your girl's mother!'

YOU LOOK LIKE A CLOWN IN THAT...

He pulls a wad of money from his pocket.

'You know, she gave me this... to kill you. And after...'

It all happens at once. A switchblade appears in his other hand, is deployed. As he finishes his sentence, something about getting Tallulah, Ms. Dern yells, 'Sailor, he's got a knife!' Like, shrieks it, like some 40s-B&W-movie-star-in-a-horror-flick shriek, and then *bam*! Sailor (for it is he) springs into action, disarming his attacker and beating him to death with his bare hands. He achieves this by smashing the man's head repeatedly against first the metal handrail at the edge of the stairs, then on the marble floor. He grips the man's head in both his hands as he does this, sweat and spit flying from him as blood spatters from the man's head. Tallulah shrieks his name twice more, loud enough to distort the sound, push the needle into the red, and a crushing heavy metal riff plays. After too long, Sailor stops, and stands panting over the body. He reaches inside his pocket and pulls out a pack of cigarettes, shaking a Marlboro out and into his mouth. He lights it with a Zippo and looks up the stairs, past Tallulah. Her mother stands at the top of the stairs, glowering at Sailor. If looks could kill. He takes the cigarette from his mouth, staining the white paper red with the blood from his hands, and points an accusing, dripping finger at her, eyes also full of hate. She makes cat claws with her fingers.

We're five minutes in. Welcome to *Wild At Heart*.

Here's the thing. I missed *Twin Peaks* on broadcast; I was just too young. And I didn't find *Blue Velvet* or *Lost Highway* until years later. So this is the first time I meet David Lynch—in what has to be his most openly juvenile movie, at the absolute perfect age to connect completely. I mean, come on—suave young rebel in a snakeskin jacket, achingly gorgeous young girlfriend, evil step-mum (is that right? It feels right), killer soundtrack, road trip, oh, and mommy's sent not one but two PI's after the kids, one of whom has ties to the weird side of organised crime, including links to some of the freakiest hitpersons you could have the misfortune of meeting. I know Nick Cage is kind of a marmite performer, and I know that's compounded by the fact that he apparently never read a script he didn't like, but here he is young and vital, and anyway, it's David Lynch, and anyway, I had never seen him before, and if he'll never be this cool again, he fucking well was this cool once, and it is glorious.

Frankly, everything about this film is glorious. Laura Dern is a revelation as Tallulah—it's a part that could so easily slip into parody, but holy shit she owns it, making her girl real, vulnerable, wonderful. There's a fear behind the eyes, and the way that feeds into her obsessive love for her man demonstrates an intelligent performance that elevates the character. Cage is captivating too, owning the screen every second the camera is on him, smouldering, laughing, crying, fighting. People bang on about the Elvis thing, and sure, that's there, explicitly, but the less mentioned but to my mind more pertinent comparison is Jimmy Dean—the car, the hair, the smokes, the dumb jacket (red leather for Dean, snakeskin for Cage). Also, there's the crack cocaine combination of beautiful vulnerability and explosively violent rage. Like Dean, he is jaw-droppingly attractive—impossibly so, like a visitor from another planet. Also like Dean, in spite of his rage, we fear for him, so clearly over his head, locked into a deteriorating orbit. We know how this story ends, and it's never good for Romeo.

And together—yes, alright, they burn up the screen, what else am I supposed to say?

Anyway, it's true, even without all the sledgehammer imagery. Yes, there's chemistry, of course, but more, there's the uncertainty, the fragility of young love. The things left unsaid, the uncomfortable silences. There's a fucking amazing scene where Sailor admits to Tallulah not only that had he known her dead father, but that he'd been present the night he'd died (in, of course, a fire). The way it plays out—him telling the story, hardly daring to look at her, her, eyes fixed outside the moving car, into the passing night—you feel the relationship shift in the moment, something bend, perhaps even break. They start the conversation in one place and finish in another, and from there the deterioration—of their story and their love—has a crushing inevitability.

I'm getting ahead of myself again. Ah, but it hardly matters. It's not quite *The Big Lebowski*, which arguably only *really* works on a second viewing, but suffice to say there's a density to the film that rewards repeat viewings. Besides, the narrative is oddly disjointed—there's a moment where one of the PI's tracking the kids (the good one, the poor doomed one) describes them leaving the hotel to the (step)mother, and we see it for a couple of seconds. At one point Tallulah sees her mother as the wicked witch in her rearview mirror, complete with broomstick and pointy hat. Oz references are scattered throughout, and again, it's not subtle, but it *does* serve as flavour, adding a surreal edge to proceedings.

So much weirdness, so much darkness, feeding into and off of each other. Mr. Reindeer, clearly the head of some kind of freak Mafia, topless young women everywhere, sitting on the toilet with a gold plated chunky mobile phone, watching a girl dance for him while he suavely takes the particulars of Marcellus Santos's hit requirements. The use of a silver dollar as the token, and its reappearance when poor doomed Johnny Faraday is shown one 'just before the act,' and how his face collapses as he realises he's been betrayed. The strange courtship between him and Tallulah's mother. The woman the kids find in a car wreck late at night, who delivers a disjointed monologue before collapsing and bleeding out—the way she continues to worry at a bleeding head wound with her finger, complaining about 'sticky stuff in her hair,' is at once heartbreaking and cringe inducing. There's an establishing shot in the street in New Orleans, and two men are walking down the street. The one furthest from the road is turned to the other, making monkey noises as they walk, while the other laughs.

Another stand out sequence occurs as the kids go to see a metal band at a club. In the mosh pit, Sailor is not so much dancing as apparently fighting off a gang of invisible ninjas when he sees someone grope his girl. With a hand gesture, he stops the band from playing, confronts the guy, and after a short but satisfying stand-off ('you look like a clown in that stupid jacket.' 'This here's a snakeskin jacket. It represents my individuality and my belief in personal freedom.' 'Asshole.') and an even shorter fight, proceeds to lead the band in a passable rendition of the Elvis track 'Treat Me Like A Fool' while the girls scream and Talullah preens and melts. It's batshit insane, and should be dreadful. It's not dreadful. It's awesome.

The weirdness and the darkness. And of course at a certain point, that darkness becomes a tailspin, as the kids run out of money and find themselves in Big Tuna, Texas. There they meet the weirdest, darkest character yet.

There, they meet Bobby Peru.

Bobby Peru is as dark a creation of cinema as I can immediately think of. Played masterfully by Willem Defoe, Bobby is a Vietnam vet with a psychotic rage that is not-really-at-all masked by his grinning, exaggerated good-cheer exterior. He is incredibly creepy from the moment he sits to drink whiskey with the kids, and when he later invites Sailor into an armed bank robbery caper, nobody, even Sailor, thinks it's a good idea. But there's a grim inevitability to the narrative by this point, and when we are party to the realisation that not only is Peru bad news on his own terms, but is actually an agent of Mr. Reindeer, there to fulfil the second part of Santos's contract, we are dismayed and upset, but not really surprised.

The robbery sequence is brilliantly handled, Lynchian in all the best meanings of the term. And given the options, things end as well as they can for

Sailor. The jump forward in time for the epilogue, in which Sailor meets his infant son, rejects Talullah, gets knocked unconscious, meets the good witch, and returns to his woman and son to declare his love in song as the credits roll again, sounds bloody awful when expressed in those terms, but is transcendent in execution. You had to be there, is what I'm trying to say.

I was there, and I'm damn grateful. I have a fairly low tolerance for the grotesque (thanks in no small part to an early exposure to the movie *Tommy*, as previously discussed), which means most Lynch is almost inaccessible for me—viewed with clenched teeth. *Wild At Heart* is toned down for him, making it just about tolerable for me, but the rage and the darkness and the weirdness and the horror and the fire all combined with my teenage brain in a most pleasing discordant symphony.

If you can ever remember feeling like you really *were Wild At Heart*, without irony or embarrassment, then this film may just get you back there for a couple of hours (of course, it may not). If that doesn't interest you, I'm sad for you.

But I'm happy for me. Because it still gets me there.

Fuck it. I'm gonna go watch it again.

ALLEGED ADULTHOOD

16+

OF WOLF AND MAN

Werewolf: The Apocalypse

For this essay, I resisted all urges to do contemporary research prior to writing—I wanted to capture as authentically as I can my memory and impressions of the subject. So the whole 'this is not journalism' thing is particularly and spectacularly apt this time. If you're interested in accuracy with regard to the subject, I'm sure there's half a dozen wikis out there—knock yourself out.

In a later essay ('Keep It Up Son, Take A Look At What You Could Have Won'), I discuss a particularly dark period of my life, and how music was one of the few threads that kept me tethered to some notion of happiness, of life as something to be lived rather than just survived. That's true, of course, but as I cast my mind back to that time, I discover, with some small surprise, that it wasn't the whole story. There was one other significant activity that I regularly partook of, with the small group of friends I lived with, which helped keep me, if not sane, at least on the right side of chronic depression.

That activity was a product of the White Wolf publishing company. A tabletop role-playing game called *Werewolf: The Apocalypse*.

This game, man. The source of my first edition rulebook is obscure *(this is a lie. I got it from the ghost)*. I know it was first edition, because there were parts where it would say, 'for more information, see page xx,' because either the extra information hadn't been added, or the copy editor hadn't picked up on the entry.

Unless there was a page xx I missed.

Shit, now that'll bug me all night.

Either way, there it was. First edition. A primer on the nature of tabletop role-playing would fall outside the scope of this project, I think, so I'll just describe it as improvised storytelling with stats and dice, and trust that if you really care and don't yet know, the internet is your friend.

What does feel 'in the scope,' however, is an overview of what *Werewolf* was like. Aside from fucking fantastic and entirely brilliant, that is.

So here's the setting for the game *Werewolf*.

Gaia is dying. Poisoned by the cancer of the spread of man and industrialisation, the planet is choking on toxins. The wilderness is dying out, strip-mined and defoliated and concreted over. The apocalypse is coming. Soon.

Into this bleak world come the player characters (PC's)—the Garou. Werewolves. Mother nature's immune system. Creatures of the Wild, who howl against the dying of the light. When Will You Rage?

I suspect I don't need to explain to you the appeal of such a game to a bunch of unemployed teenagers, living in a high unemployment area of the country in the mid-to-late 90s. To say that we could relate to the plight of characters who see the future as a black hole, crushing everything they hold sacred in an orgy of greed that will end in total destruction, would be a chronic understatement—in fact, as I reflect on this in 2020, it feels prescient, in a kind of pedestrian way. I'm sure in our minds, the only thing that separated us from the characters we played was their super-powered ability to strike back at those dark forces (albeit within the context of the knowledge that no matter what they do, things will get worse and eventually collapse—whoever created this game understood with uncanny accuracy the deep rooted cynicism of youth).

So, okay, that's the elevator pitch, but there are huge layers underneath. For starters, the Garou are divided into twelve tribes, each with its philosophies, origin myths, and allegiances. For example, there's the Silver Fangs, the aristocracy (but also possibly a little inbred), The Shadow Lords (who believe the Fangs have usurped *their* natural position of leadership and long for the opportunity to become the dominant tribe), The Black Furies, an all female tribe who consider men and male violence to be the root of the corruption (and who follow the earth mother worship and maiden/mother/crone archetypes), Bone Gnawers—transients who survive on city streets, Silent Striders—loners in a society that usually highly values the social unit of the pack—even Glass Walkers, who believe the city represents the evolution of the Wild rather than the death of it, and seek through various ways to make cities 'greener' spaces.

Underneath this is the spiritual component—the mythology of the Garou. The notion that the three forces of the universe once lived in harmony—The Wyld, pure energy and creation, The Weaver, who would knit that raw matter into order, and The

Wyrm, who would contain the excesses of both via destruction. But something went wrong; The Weaver went mad and trapped the Wyrm in his web. Now the Wyrm is also mad, twisting and thrashing in The Weavers net, bent on destroying everything, while the Wyld grows weaker and smaller.

Thing is, in the game world, this stuff isn't philosophy—it's real, tangible. The Garou have the ability to 'step sideways'—to travel into the spirit realm, the Umbra. There, the spirit servants of these forces are manifest—weaver spiders run across electricity lines and concrete buildings, toxic waste dumps writhe with twisted Wyrm spirits (called Banes) and in the deeper forests, Wydling spirits sometimes dance.

This serves at least two purposes in storytelling terms. First, obviously it opens up a whole other realm for the players to explore—like decking in Shadowrun (a cyberpunk-meets-fantasy RPG), only all the players have this ability. Secondly though, and for my mind more interestingly in storytelling terms, it removes any doubt about whether or not any of this is real—the mythology isn't relegated to past events, but is a living, breathing spirituality that players touch, taste, and can be killed by. The Apocalypse of the title is therefore also not abstract, some far away future event—it's oppressive, ever-present, breathing down the necks of the players, adding extra pain to every defeat, and quietly undermining every victory.

Yeah—no surprise it was so popular with us. Not to mention, in retrospect, good preparation for being alive in 2020.

OF WOLF AND MAN

And, in particular, popular with me. I was the Storyteller of the group (that's Games Master or Dungeon Master in old money), so my job was creating the stories, the settings, the supporting cast for the players.

I wasn't good, truth be told. I struggled to come up with original scenarios, and in fact almost exclusively used the prewritten modules that White Wolf produced—I ran the Rites Of Passage story more than once, and also had the Valkenberg Foundation book, which was a lot of fun. I made a few modifications—moving the Central Park cairn to London's Hyde Park, for example—but other than that, basically ran the game by the book.

What I enjoyed though, and what I flatter myself that I *was* good at, was character work. Character generation for my games took hours. Werewolf asks you to make a lot of decisions upfront about characters, and there's a huge list of abilities to pick from, and decisions about how many points to assign to them. And I'd make players justify every single pick, talking me through how their character had gained that skill or talent.

This wasn't, to be clear, to be a ballache. It was to really get them to think about the characters they were playing, really get to know them, inhabit them. Once we'd gone through that, each character would get their own 1-2-1 roleplay session before the main game, where I'd take them through key events in their lives, right up to their first change. These sessions were pure invention and improvisation, two minds working together to weave a narrative, create a shared reality. It was huge fun, and it meant by the

249

time we sat and played, everybody knew their story well, and was ready to dive in.

I'd also always put a Non Player Character in the pack—a werewolf character played by me. It was meant to work as a crutch, really. A way for me to manipulate the players if they got too off track, keep them at least somewhere near the narrative path I wanted them to take. In the event, I think those NPC's ended up derailing things at least as often as they helped.

But man, we had fun.

We raged against the dying of the light. We took on a Black Spiral Dancer pack in the snowy wildlands of Canada and avenged the murder of Wendigo pups. We made it to New York, and prevented a kidnapping as the streets erupted in drug fuelled violence. The Silent Strider Philadox fell in love with the deaf Ragabash Glasswalker girl, and had to leave the pack (love between Werewolves being forbidden by law, the Philadox meant to be the keepers of said law)—his replacement was a Get Of Fenris ragabash who aged in wolf years, and whose kink was killing by assassination—deeply dishonourable by Were and Get standards.

The metis Shadow Lord was slowly but surely ostracized from his tribe, even as he maintained his faith in them and their purpose. When we finished playing, he was in a coma, having sustained incredible injuries, including a collapsed lung, at the hands of a rage bane.

We gamed long into the early hours, and between us told stories of heroic despair, bravery, violence, redemption and loss. By mutual consent, in full cooperation, we carved ourselves a little alternate reality, right on the top floor living room of that crumbling shared house at the corner of a dead end street in a one horse town—not the middle of nowhere, but by God you could see it from there—and in that shithole (which I later found out escaped being condemned only because it was listed) we lived the lives of legends—creatures of wildness, rage, spirit.

We fought hard. We fought bloody. Even as the world grew darker, we tore with tooth and claw at the evil surrounding us.

And in the process, by some real world magic, we kept our own black dogs from the door.

At least sometimes. At least for a while.

I don't think you can ask for much more. Thanks, guys. For the games, for the stories, for the characters.

For the friendship.

You fucking rocked.

KEEP IT UP SON, TAKE A LOOK AT WHAT YOU COULD HAVE WON

Endless, Nameless

It's 22nd October, 1997, and my life has officially turned to shit. Having flunked out of the foundation theatre course I had been attending until July, which I only managed to beg my way onto by promising to *also* complete the BTEC in Performing Arts I had flunked out of the previous academic year by the simple expedient of doing no work whatsoever beyond the performance related exercises—and try if you can to contemplate how supremely lazy someone would have to be to actually fail a BTEC in Performing Arts—I am no longer an unemployed A-Level-equivalent student. Merely unemployed. For three years. With no qualifications beyond GCSE's, in an area of the country where youth unemployment is scary high, the wages for what shitty menial work does exist are scary low, and where beating the shit out of long haired unemployed youngsters in the town centre of a weekend lingers in that grey area between recreation and amateur sport.

Basically, I am fucked.

Also, profoundly miserable. In my conversations

KEEP IT UP SON, TAKE A LOOK AT WHAT...

since, whenever someone (usually a member of the working poor, living for the overtime and paycheck to paycheck) starts talking about the 'lifestyle choice' of living on benefits, I think back to this time. I think about how, after my top-up for housing benefit and food and yeah, okay, tobacco was paid for, I had just over £10 a week disposable income. That's for everything: clothes, toiletries, any drink that isn't tap water, books. Music. I think about how to this day, some of my most valuable-to-me albums and comics are the ones I bought during that period, where every single purchase was agonised over. And I think that it's no more a lifestyle choice than working two jobs because neither pay enough to feed your family.

No less depressing. No less soul crushing. No less grinding.

Anyway.

I'm not just broke—I'm now broke with almost no prospect of ever getting unbroke. I am basically unemployable; I have awful sleeping habits, no self-discipline, and the distinct impression that my existence is a waste of carbon. I never quite get to suicidal, but I surely bump along the bottom pretty good. No escape route from the hole I've dug myself, no clue what to do to get out. Trapped.

In holes like this, you cling to the familiar. To anything that brings you comfort. For me, that's mainly music. I listen endlessly to the LPs and cassettes I've hoarded to date, adding carefully to the collections when I spy a bargain, or one of those must-have bands puts out a new release.

The Wildhearts are one of those bands.

I bought *Earth Vs. The Wildhearts* on cassette in 1993 when I was fifteen, and it's been on heavy rotation since. In my personal pantheon of albums, it is as seminal as *Appetite For Destruction*—as classic, as vital—and I've picked up and devoured everything they've put out since, including the singles (back when £2.99 would buy you the single plus three exclusive tracks, so, you know, value for money). Looking back, their latest single sent out some warning signs—different songs on each format was a departure, but I figured they'd gotten stuck with it by a new record label. Anyway, they were still exclusive B-sides, so worth having. But the A side was a track called 'Anthem', and, erm... I didn't get it.

On a fairly epic scale. And the rest of the B-sides, while more clearly songs as opposed to walls of noise, were similarly red line distorted beyond being listenable to. 'Oops,' remarked one of my friends on first listen. No longer living at home, that lifeline to new music discovery that was *Kerrang!* Magazine was closed to me, so I had no way of reading advance reviews.

But it was The Wildhearts. Clearly the single was a goof.

There's no way they'd do a whole album like that.

So when *Endless, Nameless* arrived at Our Price, I plunked down my money for the week with little hesitation. By God, I could do with a new Wildhearts record in my life, those poppy punky angry happy tunes and lyrics. Bring it on.

And, I mean, fuck. I knew there were problems before I got home. Opening the cassette box on the

KEEP IT UP SON, TAKE A LOOK AT WHAT...

way back, the inlay card had the lyrics printed in it. This was a massive departure for The Wildhearts—prior releases just had artwork and band info, never the words. My mind skipped back to the wall of noise that was *Anthem*, and my heart sank. I looked up the words, figuring I'd at least understand what they were singing in that fucking chorus. 'I'm in love with the rock 'n roll world.' What the fuck does that mean?

By the time I got it home, I was really, really nervous. I played the tape. It was the same distorted noise, and also too quiet, the levels way down. I turned it up, way up.

I listened to the whole album.

I went and got my friend—another Wildhearts fanatic.

I sat him down, and we smoked and listened to it, not talking.

When it finished playing, I turned to him. I remember feeling almost choked up, like someone I thought was a friend had mugged me. Thinking about the money I'd spent, could not unspend.

He looked at me.

'I think that was fucking awful. And fucking brilliant.'

We sat, looking at each other. Then he said, 'Play it again.'

I did.

I basically haven't stopped.

I listened. With the words, without the words. Soaking it in. Straining to hear through the distortion to the songs, the lyrics. And gradually, it opened up to me, started to speak. And once it started, it was like a light bulb flickering into life.

This was a horror album.

It was everything The Wildhearts had been to date, with all the polish, the varnish, the love of melody and crispness blistered off by sheer blazing fury and despair. The whole album was basically like 'Greetings from Shitsville' from *Earth Vs.* Except this time, there was no escape, no way out. It was the sound of someone utterly trapped, entombed by the weight of their crushing poverty and misery, howling into the sky. It was the sound of despair so total that it didn't even give a fuck if you could hear it. It wasn't a cry for help so much as a primal scream of 'fuck you' to a world turned irredeemably hostile.

It was one of the best fucking rock 'n roll albums of the nineties, maybe the best. And nobody has fucking heard it, and of those that have, most hate it. That's fine. It's even fitting. But I'm here to tell you that from where I was, at the lowest point of my life, seeing no bright stars anywhere, starting to suspect the light at the end of the tunnel was an oncoming train, this album saved my life. It's not the record that got me back on my feet, or the one that I heard the day I realised that not only could I leave town, but I had to, if I was going to have any kind of shot at happiness—but it saved me from the darkest moments, with the simplest possible message.

You are not alone.

Out there, somewhere, a man you respect and admire and hero worship a bit, a man who is living the rock star life you have only ever, will only ever, dream of, somewhere that man is hurting every bit as bad as you and more. He's feeling every inch of the despair and hopelessness and impotent rage you are.

KEEP IT UP SON, TAKE A LOOK AT WHAT...

And he's poured it out into a wall of sound, and that sound is now in the room with you, and you are not alone.

You can keep 'Everybody Hurts'. *This* is my fucking faith.

Later, I'd learn all about the horrific biographical problems that lead to the recording of this album. But really, it's there on the tracks. You don't need a translator.

A record named after the secret track on an album made by a heroin addict rock star who would later blow his own brains out with a shotgun. Not exactly subtle. Except it is, somehow. Its excesses are so violent, so near total, it requires an act of endurance to listen past the noise and hear the raw beating heart underneath.

Make that effort, though, focus hard, really fucking listen, and the rewards are there in spades, and all the sweeter for the trying. For starters, as dark as it is, it's also hilarious.

Seriously.

Start with the song titles—'Junkenstien', 'Nurse Maximum', 'Pissjoy'. 'Thunderfuck', for heaven's sake. And it's not just wry, surface level gags; this is a rich vein that runs through the whole record. 'Junkenstien', for instance, starts with levels recorded intentionally too quiet, and then gradually steps up each pattern change, so it's at normal volume when you get to the second verse. Which means if you're anything like me, you're actually listening to it at blistering volume, because you turned it up to hear the opening. It's a genius way to get you to listen to the record at the volume intended by the artist, but it's also kind of a practical joke, too.

'Nurse Maximum' comes off as a love song to Nurse Ratchet from *Cookoo's Nest*. 'Anthem' is a bitter, blistering assault on the notion of the Big Rock Song, but it's also a pisstake of the same, what with the distortion turned up to fifteen, and *that* chorus. The gaggle of children delightedly scream-singing 'Piss! Joy! Na-na-na-na-na!' during the chorus of *that* song is just glorious, a reminder of how joyful it is to be a child and swearing. The section of 'SoundDog Babylon' that drops into a sub-Stone Roses limp grove, before revving back up to that hyper chorus is similarly humorous, in a just-because-we-can kind of way.

And then there is 'Now Is The Colour'.

This is the one where it all comes together, for me. Because it's all in here, in the lyric and the pile driver repeated riff, the teeth-gritting percussion and the screaming chorus. It's furious, and ugly, and desperate, and bleak, but it's also a joke, a goof, a punchline:

Hey there sweet thing, cop a class A,
You've got to keep illegal while the kids are away,
It tastes a lot better when you know it's a crime,
Now is the Colour, and Blue is the Time...

And so on. It's relentless, raging, the energy borne of desperation and fever. It's mesmerising. It's transcendent. It's the clearest illustration I can immediately think of for the gulf between representation of music as notes on a page, and the reality of what a performance can sound like, what it can make you feel. Every time I get to that collapsing end, as the guitar crashes to silence and the sirens wail and the news reporter rattles on incoherently, I'm left fucking stunned. Every single time.

Just over a year before, Marilyn Manson's seminal *Antichrist Superstar* had been released. I'd initially resisted it, but was eventually won over (as I'll discuss in more detail in *Volume II*)—inevitably, really. It's intelligent, extraordinary well produced, apparently unhinged noise actually perfectly performed and managed, structurally smart, lyrically dense, and pleasingly nihilistic. It's the soundtrack to the end of the world. Or more accurately, the soundtrack to a slick Hollywood movie about the end of the world. That's not so much a bug as a feature, mind—Manson has always had one eye on the mainstream, and his place in pop culture, and he's as much in love with the American dream/nightmare that he interrogates as he is perplexed by it—as much a product as a producer of product. And *Antichrist Superstar* remains a superb, superlative metal album.

But *Endless, Nameless* shits all over it from a great height.

There are several important reasons why, but in essence they all boil down to the same related factors—authenticity and class.

Because Ginger Wildheart didn't have, or aspire to, a house on the Hollywood hills. He was just an almost supernaturally gifted songwriter with mental health issues who went, as with so many of his peers, untreated and undiagnosed. He was a man living life at the bleeding edge, not because it was cool, or edgy, or to be the next big thing, but because he had no fucking choice. He was born to work this job, born to make music—anyone who's spent any time with *Earth Vs.* can tell you that as a moral certainty. But turns out that the music industry in the 90s is actually kind of a desolate and dangerous place for someone gifted but vulnerable—I know, shocker, right?

See, Manson's angst and misery is that of a middle class kid, ultimately. By which I mean, it's the ennui of someone who had his material needs met, but still feels a gaping hole in his life, one that can't be filled by drugs or God or sex. It's music written by someone smart enough to know they've won the genetic lottery, being born to the country and class and race that he has, but also smart enough to realise it's still a crock of shit, and feel the roaring emptiness at the heart of that existence.

And I say that not to denigrate. That's a real thing—the feeling that you should be grateful, but you're still the ugliest and most awkward kid in the class, the one nobody can relate to, the disconnect and alienation—people get killed over that feeling. To have the courage to put that into words and sound for all us misfits is a good thing. As fellow Gingernutter Duncan Ralston reminded me on Facebook, similar things are also true of NiN's *The Downward Spiral*—another fine, bleak album of the 90s.

But it doesn't touch the sides of the misery and despair of *Endless, Nameless*. *Endless, Nameless* is the sound of a man choking on his ambitions. It's the sound of a man who's just fallen in love with crack cocaine, knows it is likely to kill him, and cannot stop. It is the sound of a man who has lived the dream, only to find it to be a waking nightmare from which there is no escape. It is the sound of that man screaming into the darkness, howling into the void, doing the only thing that makes sense to him, as pained and broken as he is. Doing the one thing he can do, must do, the one thing that even the smack can't kill.

Making music. Turning feelings into sounds.

Endless, Nameless is the sound of the abyss. No more, no less. It's not for everyone. It's ragged and distorted, and yeah, in places even broken.

It's also a fucking spectacular album. A work of art.

In a way, I'm glad it's obscure, even hated by many diehard fans. It should be. It's hard to listen to, and it does not give a fuck if you like it.

But if this record does speak to you, then sister, brother, I feel you.

I feel you.

PS—If you only listen to one track from the album, make it 'Now Is The Colour'. I can't promise it will change your life. But it's possible.

GIVE ME A CHANCE TO APOLOGISE, OKAY?

Sleepers

There's a ghost haunting *My Life in Horror*. He doesn't haunt all the entries, but a few. Yes, quite a few. I know a big part of what I'm doing with this series of essays is circling that ghost wearily. Finding ways to talk about him without talking about him.

So tonight I'm going to talk about the most disturbing book I've read.

In a break with tradition, I'm not going to play the usual shell game either. The book is called *Sleepers*, and it's by Lorenzo Carcaterra. I've only read it once. I can't imagine I will ever put myself through it again. Beyond using Google to get the author's name, I'm not revisiting the text at all. That said, if your stomach and will are strong, and descriptions of abuse won't trigger you, I'd recommend it, I think. I cannot remember a more intense reading experience. And yeah, there was a movie. I've heard it's good, but if you haven't, I wouldn't. There's no fucking way it can beat the source.

And I'm about to spoil the hell out of it, so if you don't know and you want to find out for yourself—last chance.

It's oh, 1998 or '99. I am somewhere between

twenty and twenty-one, and while life is better than it was back in my *Endless, Nameless* days, it's still not good. Having reached the sensible conclusion that if I don't leave my college town, I will be buried there, I'm sleeping in a spare room of a friend's house in London. My memory is that I'm not yet working in the pub that will later inspire my long short story *The Debt* and the protagonist from *Lifeline* (see *Volume II* for more), so it's probably '98. And I'm suffering one of my periodic insomnia bouts. Worse, I have nothing to read. So I go to my friend's room and peruse his bookcase, eventually pulling off the shelf the black cover paperback, with the title picked out in white typeset on the spine.

It begins with a statement that this is a true story, with names and details changed. Later, I'd wonder about that a lot. It seems to me that you'd have to change one whole hell of a lot of details to avoid landing someone connected with this book in jail, but as far as I know there have been no prosecutions. At the same time, the story rings truer than any autobiography I've read, save that of Jim Thompson himself. So who knows? I'm sure Google would tell me, but I don't want to know.

From there we meet our four kids. Street kids, essentially—working class, 1960s, Hell's Kitchen, New York, New York. My memory is Italian American, which the author's name would seem to back up. Catholic. And absolutely not saints, that's clear. Tearaways. Petty street crime. I can't remember the ages with clarity, but I have them around twelve or thirteen—old enough to kid themselves they were teenagers, but still really kids.

And we get a few pages to meet them, their personalities, their street rips and dumb scams. It's exhilarating, in an ominous way.

Then they do a terrible thing.

They steal a hotdog cart. There is a pursuit. And then, at the top of some subway steps, they lose control of the cart. It falls down the stairwell, and it kills a man.

They kill a man.

And I mean, in the narrative, it's horrible. The guilt and the fear are palpable. They go to their local priest (played by De Niro in the movie, I understand) and confess, and snot and cry and beg and just about shit themselves with fear. And it's possible you're thinking, 'What about the victim?' and if you are, I'm not going to tell you you're wrong. They took a life, and that's terrible. It was an accident, sure, but they took irresponsible actions, and those actions had horrific consequences.

You may think they deserve everything they get.

You may.

But you'd be wrong.

My memory is the priest gets them to turn themselves in. That feels right. He does this not without misgivings. There is, of course, a trial. The children plead guilty, express remorse. Certainly the author is remorseful—his guilt is palpable.

The judge—is there history, with the priest, real or implied? Or the prosecutor? I can't remember for sure. What I do know is that they don't get suspended sentences. They get convicted of manslaughter, and sent to a tough 'kid prison'—reformatory? Something like that.

GIVE ME A CHANCE TO APOLOGISE, OKAY?

And the priest, he knows. He knows what they are about to face. He tries to council them. Be brave, he says. Be brave, be hurt, but don't become hard.

Don't go hard.

And that's it. The four get shipped out. I think. Maybe one of them did get suspended. It would make sense, given what follows, but I can't recall. It's kind of overshadowed by where they end.

And, I mean, on one level it's indistinguishable from grownup jail. There's shitty food, there's guards in uniforms, there's cells and PT and lights out and lockdown and solitary, and all the shit you'd expect from any prison movie you'd care to name.

The only difference is that here, the guards are a gang of vicious sadists.

It starts with a scene you'll recall from the movie, if you've seen it—one of the boys is viciously beaten at a mealtime, causing him to drop his food. He is then made to eat the food from the floor. With his hands.

And okay, look, cards on the table—it won't come as any galloping shock to anyone who has so much as glanced at my author photo that your humble correspondent has issues when it comes to figures of authority. There is very little in life that will more readily make me angry, raging, sick-to-the-stomach snarling like the abuse of authority.

And, of course, that anger comes from where anger always comes: fear.

Violence frightens me. Pain frightens me. The knowledge that I live in a society where I could, theoretically, be put in prison, terrifies the shit out of me. The concept of jail is a horror. Yes, of course because I'm not 6'2" and built like a brick shithouse, yes because I'd be at very high risk of assault. All of that. But/and/also, because on a base psychological level, the notion that I'd be at the utter whim and mercy of armed men in uniforms makes my mind want to shut down. It may not be my worst nightmare, but it's on the top three for sure, and I couldn't immediately tell you what the other two are.

So given all this, you can already see why this book has me by the scruff of the neck. Skin crawling. Throat closing. Heart pounding.

Then the guards, three of them, maybe four, take the kid from his cell that night, off to a private location. And they orally rape him.

That pretty much sets the tone for the next hundred, hundred and fifty pages. The kids are beaten, raped, abused, mistreated. Over and over and over again. The guards claim that the sexual violence is being meted out as punishment for infractions, but it becomes increasingly clear as events unfold that they're simply doing it because they can.

It's a blur, and honestly not helped by some of the overlap with *Shawshank Redemption*, given how many damn times I've seen that fucking movie, but *Shawshank* is like the Disneyland version of this story, and this is the full blooded Brian De Palma uncut version.

Based on a true story.

From the long, numbing litanies of abuse and degradation, there is one thing that stands out—burned irrevocably into my memory as sure as a scar.

Every year, there's a football match. American Football. Officially, 'touch' or 'flag' football, where physical contact is equal to a tackle. The public and

GIVE ME A CHANCE TO APOLOGISE, OKAY?

press are invited, to witness this showcase of reform in action—good all-American fun. The kicker? It's guards vs. inmates.

I guess by this point I'm stating the brutally obvious, but the guards always win.

So this particular year, our narrator talks to the kid who is currently the leader of the black youth in the institution, and tries to talk him into actually playing the football game. Playing to win. And the conversation goes something like this:

Narrator: So let's do it, man. Let's play them. Let's *beat* them!

Leader: You want me to tell my people to actually play the game? Not just throw it like every year?

N: Yeah!

L: You know they'll probably win anyway, right? I mean, one of them will be the damn ref.

N: I know...

L: And you know if by some miracle we *do* actually win this thing, they are going to make our lives a living hell, right?

N: Yeah, I know it.

L: And you still want me to do this thing?

N: I still want you to do it.

L: Why? Why in the hell should I do this crazy thing?

N: Because fuck them. That's why.

I feel so much, here. So much.

There's the empathic anger, surging at the injustice, wanting to hit back. There's the terror—of acting, of doing this crazy and dangerous thing, and the repercussions. I want them to do it. I don't want them to do it. My eyes are bleary with tiredness, but I've never felt less like sleeping. I want them to do it for them. For me. I want vengeance, even if pyrrhic. I want the guards to feel just a touch of the humiliation and shame of their victims. I want it so badly I can taste it. And I am also bitterly, powerfully afraid for them. It's an incredibly potent cocktail, and the memory keeps me up past my bedtime, now as then, reliving the trauma of a child I have never met, will never know.

The description of the match is blow-by-blow, and largely incomprehensible to me, American Football being then an utterly alien sport. What I do know is that the guards fight dirty, the ref cheats outrageously... and the kids still manage to win.

I think it's the nearest I've come to understanding how one might feel a savage joy at victory in combat. I mean, I've never personally experienced it, except in retrospect. The few physical fights I've been in, win or lose, were always adrenaline and a kind of hyper-aware calm, followed by shakes, tears, and the urge to vomit. It's only once the events have become history that I can look back with pride or shame at how I handled myself.

But reading this story, I felt something savage surge in my chest. Something that was fundamentally unconcerned with fairness, or justice, though it used both words. The feeling was simply a vicious triumph, of teeth grinding, rage filled... joy? No. Too heavy for that. Too ugly, too mean. It felt great and strong and horrible and sickening all at once. I don't think I've ever felt anything like it, before or since.

GIVE ME A CHANCE TO APOLOGISE, OKAY?

You can well imagine how the crash felt.

Because, of course, for the crime of winning, and humiliating the guards, our narrator is beaten. Badly. Then put into solitary, for—fuck, *Shawshank* interferes here again, but a long damn time. And when he gets out, he finds out that the kid he'd talked into this madness went one better—they beat him to death.

I remember crying. I remember thinking that in any sane, just world, we'd all know the name of this kid. There would be statues to him in every city of the globe. He'd be a martyr. The day of his death would be holy, a day of quiet reflection and rededication to fighting corruption and violence-as-authority. We would remember, and our hearts would fill with righteous rage, and we'd each of us vow to do everything to go forth and make sure this never, ever happened again.

How do we forget this? How do *I* forget this?

Anyway.

There's more abuse, more pain and humiliation, but eventually the kids get out. Our narrator is released before his friends. On his last night, he is taken to the private place, and made to watch the guards abusing the friends he is leaving behind. They remind him they will continue to do this while he is on the outside.

Amazingly, the story doesn't end there.

Our narrator gets out. He seeks out the priest, tells him what has happened. He cries. He has nightmares. He experiences night terrors and bedwetting and, well, all the PTSD shit you'd expect. But he remembers the priest's warning, and he does not grow hard.

His friends are not so lucky. By the time they get out, he sees that something fundamental has changed in them. There is a coldness at their core, now. A hardness. They become part of the mob, killers.

And then there's the other kid. He becomes a lawyer.

And here's the part where my refusal to go back is going to fuck this up. I think... No, I got it. He becomes a public prosecutor. Yes, that's right, he works for the DA.

So when the two mob kids, now fully grown hard men, locate and shoot down the head guard in cold blood, he ends up prosecuting the case.

And if your bullshit detector just went off, well, I hear you. This is what I meant up top about how you've got to change a bit more than the names to make this shit fly. Because what this guy does is manipulate the prosecution in such a way that, while ostensibly running things to the best of his ability, he's subtly undermining his case.

And then comes the *piece de resistance*.

Our narrator manages to meet with the defence lawyers. And he hands them a big fat dossier that lists all the allegations, testimonies, and evidence that points to the systemic sexual abuses perpetrated by the murder victim. It's devastating, and transforms the chances of the defendants. It's at this point that one of the defence attorneys, reading through this dossier that at a stroke destroys a man's character and legacy irrevocably, turns to the narrator and utters what is, for my money, the single greatest recorded moment of spoken dialogue in human history:

GIVE ME A CHANCE TO APOLOGISE, OKAY?

'Do me a favour, will you? If I ever piss you off, give me a chance to apologise, okay?'

Goosebumps, even now.

And of course they pull it off, and the killers are set free, found not guilty. And of course, in a very real sense, it doesn't matter. Not just because some things cannot be made right—though there is that. But also, the killers are still killers, and the life they have chosen still destroys them. I'm reminded of the Henry Hill commentary track on the DVD of *Goodfellas*, where, during that long panning shot of the bar where Liotta via voiceover introduces the mob to us ('Mickey Four Eyes, Tommy Two-Times, etc...'), on the commentary track, Henry Hill (the real life, actual Henry Hill) says, 'This, right here, this is why I love the FBI. Because aside from me, every single person in this scene is dead now, or in jail.' These kids-turned-killers are never going to find the FBI, and their fate is inevitable.

But I'm also reminded of one of my all-time favourite movies, *The Sting* (which I'm about to spoil, so for fuck's sake go and watch it if you haven't already, it's one of the best movies ever made. Almost as good as *RoboCop*.) At the very end, having successfully conned the vicious gangster who had murdered his friend out of hundreds of thousands of 1930s dollars, Hooker (Robert Redford) turns to his mentor, Henry Gondorff (Paul Newman), his face still and grave, and after a pause says, 'You're right. It's not enough.'

The two con men regard each other, Newman's too-blue eyes burning up the screen.

Then Hooker's face splits into a grin that goes

all the way to his boots, as he says, 'But... it's close!'

They laugh.

And it might all be bullshit. Like I say, I haven't looked it up—I won't—but it's very hard to swallow the notion that the case is not identifiable—that the prosecutor can't be found, and held accountable for perverting the course of justice. Maybe the ending is false, and maybe Hooker's grin and laugh is false too—maybe he's just giving Gondorff what he needs. He is, after all, a conman. It's possible.

It's possible.

But as with *The Sting*, *Sleepers* is a perfect revenge story—and unlike *The Sting*, claims to be true.

And I want to believe. Because some things can't be put right.

But that doesn't mean we shouldn't try.

WHY DON'T YOU LIE BACK AND ENJOY BEING INFERIOR?

Last House on the Left

I'd always planned to talk about this movie. When I sent Jim a list of proposed subjects for this column, I'm sure this film was on the first page. But I'm not going to lie; I wasn't in a hurry. This one profoundly bothered me. Anyhow. I figured there was no hurry. Would that I'd been right about that. Do yourself a favour, I beg ya—if there's some creative force in your life, some actor or director or writer or singer that means something to you, speak out on it while they're still drawing breath. Regret being a gushing idiot. It's better than the alternative.

Guilty confession time—I'm actually kind of a wimp when it comes to horror movies. I like the idea of extreme and exploitation cinema, but watching it? Not so much. For some reason, for all that I could watch *Die Hard* or *RoboCop* from now until the end of time, depictions of violence that seem more realistic turn my stomach. In fact, they turn my *mind*. Some internal part pulls away, horrified, sickened. Actually, now I think about it, *RoboCop* is the first movie I can remember making me feel that way— Murphy's execution is bloody, sustained, and brutal, not to mention cruel and sadistic. It still provokes a physical response when I see it now, some one hundred plus viewings in: increased heart rate, a feeling like my throat has swollen, a prickle of fear sweat. Listen to any episode of 'Watching RoboCop' if you don't believe me; you'll hear my reaction, damn near every time. It's fucking horrible, not to put too fine a point on it.

So given this low tolerance, I've avoided exploitation horror. I'm glad the form exists, and I enjoy blogs like the excellent Film Gutter on *Gingernuts Of Horror*—not least because it means I can gain insight about this genre without having to watch the films. But *Hostel* never appealed, let alone *I Spit On Your Grave*. In fact, strictly between you and me, I haven't yet managed to sack up enough to watch *The Texas Chainsaw Massacre*. Even *House Of 1000 Corpses* took a couple of attempts. By and large, I've given the genre a healthy respectful distance.

With one notable exception.

It is the mid 2000s. I am burning through my twenties at an alarming rate, the way you do when you're too young to know better. For reasons now obscure, I'm staying with a friend in Sacramento, California. We've rented a stack of videos from Tower Video—*the* Tower Video, as my friend insists on reminding me. To the best of my recollection, the conversation went like this:

'You really liked the *Elm Streets* as a kid, right?'

'Yeah. *Scream*, as well. First horror movie I saw at the cinema.' (see *Volume II* for more on both of these.)

'Want to see his first movie? The villain is called Freddie Krug.'

'No shit?'

'Yeah. Don't know if there's any similarities with Freddie, but…'

'Sure, stick it on the pile.'

And that is how I ended up seeing *Last House On The Left*. For the first and last time.

And no, we're no longer friends.

So, that sick sweat I talked about earlier? Oh yeah. In spades. I remember little of the dialogue, to be honest—I had to look up the pull quote I used as the title for this article on IMDB. I do remember the 'plot', such as it is. And to jump to the end, the way the villains eventually meet their grisly fate certainly made me wince. There's also an utterly vicious swipe at the police, the callousness with which they are portrayed as bumbling idiots rings in memory to this day as being genuinely shocking in its pull-no-punches delivery. So of course, there's all that and almost certainly much more.

But that's not what this movie is about to me.

No, what this movie is about to me is two girls being held at gunpoint. Two girls stuck in the woods with a gang of sexual sadists using them as meat puppets. The terror, the constant quiet sobbing as the two are stripped, metaphorically and literally. The utter indifference on the part of their captors, the cold amusement.

There's a moment, as the girls are being ordered to do things to each other—make out, and later slap each other—when one of them says to the other, 'Please, just… remember it's me. It's me. I love you.' I can feel a lump in my throat thinking about it. And behind it, a hint of gorge too. It's fucking horrible, and it feels like it goes on for hours. The orders grow increasingly sadistic, and the girls sobbing compliance more desperate and abject. And there are no rules, out here—literally—in the woods. We've abandoned any pretence at 'normal' movie narrative, even normal horror movie tropes. There's no larger than life monster—just a small pack of dull, vicious sadists. There's no white knight, no obvious 'final girl'. The rhythm is also utterly broken—we're about a third of the way in, is my memory, and suddenly we're just stuck in real time, in this grotesque yet banal scene of violent coercion. The cops aren't coming. No one is coming. The girls know it. There's no way to fight. No higher authority to appeal to. No cunning plan or concealed weapon. None of the things a trapped heroine always has in a situation like this.

There are no rules. The rules are all broken. And in their absence... cruelty. Debasement. Pain and humiliation, ever increasing by hellish degree. The only promise, the only certainty, that it will continue to escalate, to get worse, more vile, more violent, until the dull sociopaths become bored enough to finish you off for good. No escape from the fear or pain. No way to deflect or disassemble.

No way out.

I don't know about you, but I have a hard time coming up with a purer essence of horror than that notion. Certainly when I think about my list of fears, being utterly at the mercy of a stupid but skilled sadist has to be a serious contender for the top spot. And in this movie, there is no looking away, no escape—as the viewer, you are trapped in the woods with these sociopaths and their victims.

WHY DON'T YOU LIE BACK AND ENJOY...

Wes Craven doesn't look away, and neither can you.

I haven't looked into the making of the film, so I don't know how much was on the page and how much was improvised or directed. I do remember it feeling raw and naturalistic to an excruciating degree. And, in a way, it doesn't matter, does it? Whether it was a brilliantly crafted script, or Mr. Craven simply knew how to get the best out of his cast, the end result is the same—as nasty a slice of cinema as I'm ever likely to see.

You'll have gathered from the above that this film fucked me up pretty badly. I'll almost certainly never watch it again. But then, as you'll also gather from the above, I really don't need to. The film, or at least the impression of the film, is etched across my brain, a small but permanent scar.

I don't know if that makes it great art, but I think it does make it something. *Last House On The Left* is gratuitously unpleasant and nihilistic, but it is also unarguably possessed of its own sick, fevered energy. Now almost a half-century old, it still has a power to shock and disturb that few pictures since can match. Not because it's a devastatingly intelligent piece of writing (though it's far, far smarter than its reputation). Not because it's brilliantly shot, or the effects work is eye-popping. Nope, this puppy does it the old fashioned way—by looking long and deep and unblinkingly at the darkest lights that human beings are capable of carrying. By staring into the abyss, and then daring you to look away.

I couldn't. I didn't. And it changed me. And while

I'll never watch the movie again, I wouldn't unwatch it for the world.

Some things have to be endured. And sometimes, the only way to find the edge is to go over it. Wes Craven went all the way over it, first time out. I love the ferocity and courage that must have taken. I salute it. And I salute him. Whatever else he was or wasn't, Wes Craven fucking made *Last House On The Left*. If he'd done nothing else with his life, he deserves celebration and respect for that.

As it happens, he did a lot more. *Volume II* will engage at some length with the work and legacy of Mr. Craven. Freddy was *the* movie bogyman of my childhood, every bit as much as The Wolfman or Christopher Lee's Dracula were for previous generations. I am excited about the notion of revisiting *Elm Street*, and as I noted near the top, *Scream* also holds a very special place in my own personal rite of passage.

But on the day Wes Craven passed, it feels fitting to remember one of my last experiences with his work. The first movie he made. A slice of horror so unremittingly bleak, such a pure expression of nihilism, that I just can't face ever watching it again.

You will be missed, Wes. Rest in peace. And thank you for making movies that disturbed my rest.

OUR LIFE IN HORROR

Eagles of Death Metal / Queen at Hyde Park

It's the 14th November, 2015, and I've awoken from a very private nightmare into a very public one. Once more, a small number of men of violence have transformed a major city centre on a Friday night from a place of bustling activity, celebration, and drunken idiocy into a bloodbath. I can't say I'm numb, exactly. Not quite numb. Sickened? Scared? Yeah, a bit. I feel… outraged. Hurt. I feel like *I've* been attacked, somehow.

Which in many important ways is bullshit and selfish and narcissistic in the extreme. For starters, horror shows like this are happening all over the world every day, and are not only not breaking, 'we-interrupt-our-regular-programing' type news—they're not news at all. Because they're happening Somewhere Else, often to people whose skin tone is darker than mine happens to be. And if you're reading this and thinking that on any level, yes, you are right, and I own the hypocrisy, and am shamed by it. It's perhaps the ultimate and darkest and most poisonous expression of privilege.

But it doesn't change how I feel.

And right now, I feel quite a bit like I'm reeling from the emotional equivalent to a crowbar to the head. Stunned. Disoriented. Dislocated, mood swinging between fury and a sadness so deep it borders on despair.

Grief too. Grief for the parents whose children have just been filled with bullets, executed for the mortal crime of liking *The Eagles Of Death Metal*. Children without parents, too, undoubtedly. Lovers, families, friends, workplaces, all facing a gaping bloody wound in their lives where once walked someone they knew. And yes, absolutely, also grief for the many, many innocent Muslims who will now feel the need to hold their children that much closer, and fear the outside world that much more. And then there are the thousands fleeing the utter carnage and brutality of the Syrian civil war, already cowering in abject conditions having fled a horror beyond the comprehension of most, who now face victimisation by a grotesque right wing that never lets a good crisis go to waste when they have a chance to further their own vile, nihilistic, blood soaked agenda. Grief, always. Grief most of all.

And yes, this takes place in a context. France has struggled with how to assimilate and accommodate its Muslim population for some time, and it has not always acquitted itself with honour, to put it mildly. I do not seek to justify, excuse, or apologise for the actions of these murderers. They are vile, base fascists, and beneath contempt. To seek to understand is never, ever, to excuse. At the same time, if we don't learn from history, we are doomed to repeat it.

And I do feel so very doomed right now. Like many of you, I am sure, I find myself thinking back. To 9/11. To 7/7. To Madrid. And of course to Paris, less than twelve months ago, when homicidal fascists decided their feelings were more important than the lives of those they disagreed with.

Fascism is the word, incidentally—for ISIS and all the criminals they inspire. Islamofascism is not only a redundancy, in my opinion, but actively misleading. These people have far, far more in common with Hitler and his ideology than they do with the religion of Islam. No, like the KKK, and for identical reasons, they are Nazis, pure and simple. I deny these criminals the dubious legitimacy of veiling their crimes in a religious garb: they are Nazi thugs, whose only ideology is destruction, bloody death, and pain. Fuck them, and fuck everything they stand for. And also, understand this: this is no more about religion than Columbine was about Marilyn Manson.

Each time something like this happens, I find myself back in this numbed mindset. Unable to process. Wildly absorbing the horrors, compulsively glued to news feeds, somehow hoping the flood of information will cohere, will form a narrative that allows me to make sense of what I am seeing.

So far, no luck.

And this one feels... especially personal. I genuinely didn't think I could feel worse than I did after the *Charlie Hebdo* shooting. As someone who feels like the most important role I play, after those of husband and father, is that of a creative, someone who turns feelings into words, the notion that a sincere expression of art could lead to being murdered offended me to the core. I know that *CH* is a 'problematic publication', incidentally, especially when viewed in the wider context of the treatment of France's Muslim population by the body politic. And France has a strong nationalist party that has a genuinely uncomfortable level of support amongst the general population. Freely acknowledging all that, I remain horrified, on a level that I can barely express, that satire should be responded to with bullets. Since that day, my FB cover has been a picture of pencils bearing the words, 'This machine kills fascists.' I can't imagine that I will ever take it down.

Still, we may have topped it with this one. A new depth may just have been plumbed. Because here's the thing—I am not a religious person. I'm not much of any kind of man of faith. Doubt, skepticism, and uncertainty are my constant companions. I find myself, for the most part, alienated by tribalism. I am a member of a political party, but that was a long time coming, and truthfully, it's still something I feel uncomfortable and conflicted about.

And until recently, there was only one exception to this, really, and that exception was music.

I've been a fan of rock and metal since I was eleven, and it's the nearest thing I have to a tribal allegiance. I have the long hair (receding at a rapid rate but still, for now, intact), the battered leather biker jacket, and more black T-shirts with band logos on than I can count.

Music is my tribe. Music is the nearest I have to a religion. And a live gig is the nearest I come to church.

I've been to many, many amazing shows over the years, and the thing that sticks with me the most is the unwritten Law of The Mosh Pit. Simply put, this is the mutual understanding between all metalheads, punks and rockers, and the understanding is this: in the pit, you go as crazy as you want—pogo, slam, bounce, circle mosh, whatever. The floor is yours, and everyone is fair game for a shoulder barge or push. If you can't stand the heat, get the fuck out of the pit.

And that stands right up to the moment that someone falls over.

As soon as that happens, the Law of The Pit is clear—if you see someone fall, you pull them back up.

I've seen it, time and time and time again. In Glasgow, watching Slipknot on their first UK tour, at Marilyn Manson in Manchester, Rancid at Brixton Academy. Sepultura, 1999, Big Day Out, Milton Keynes Bowl, 60,000 screaming metalheads, one of the most insane pits I've witnessed. Giant skinheads, red faces twisted with rage and dripping with sweat, stinking and heaving and bashing and swinging their arms around like they are karate fighting invisible enemies. I was right in there, feeling that elemental heat, the crush, the energy... and one of those guys knocked me clear off my feet. Before I'd even hit the deck, his arm grabbed mine, pulled me back up. His face had cleared instantly, and he looked just like... well, Dave from accounts, maybe. 'You alright?' Big grin. 'Yeah, fine!' 'Cool!' and he's back off into the carnage.

That's my tribe. These are my people.

This is my church.

So the notion that my tribe, my church, is considered a target for fascists... Yeah. Fuck you guys.

Because I've been here before. 08/07/05. I have tickets to see Queen and Paul Rodgers at Hyde Park.

I know the show has been cancelled, after the previous days attacks, but I've booked the day off and the train ticket anyway, and two of my dearest friends, who I am going to the show with, are living in London, so fuck it. I go anyway. And when I get to Euston, I buy a tube ticket and head down without a pause.

Because fuck them. They don't get to win.

The gig is postponed a week, but when it does happen, it's magnificent. He's no Freddie, but Mr. Rodgers gives a decent account of himself, and hey, it's Brian May and Roger Taylor, and they're as good as you might expect.

And then, over halfway through, something amazing happens. Roger alludes to the events of the previous weekend, and dedicates a song ('written by the second greatest songwriter the UK ever produced,' which made me chuckle) to all of us.

Then 2005 Queen play 'Imagine'.

Not a dry eye in the house. Then or now.

These are my people. This is my tribe. All races, all genders, all religions and none. Absolutely all welcome. Standing together. United in a shared moment of love for life itself.

Fuck you, fascists. You don't get anywhere near this. You don't get to stop this, or curtail it.

It's going to be bad for a while, now. Innocent Muslims will be targeted by bigots. Refugees will be treated with suspicion and fear. It will be harder to leave those war zones than it already is. And people who should know better will talk about this as a 'war', which is a) factually inaccurate, and b) playing right into the hands of the enemy.

Because the whole fucking point is, this isn't a war. Neither the 'combatants' nor the victims are soldiers. So by definition, it's not a war.

It's a crime. And it requires a criminal justice response. To do otherwise is to play into the hands of apocalyptic mad men who want a religious war. Call me old fashioned, but I'd say one of the first principles of winning any kind of conflict would be denying your opponents their goals.

Still, it'll be hard. Travel will be tougher again for a while. Gigs security will have to step up, with all the inconveniences you'd expect. An open society with freedom of movement is always vulnerable in this way. And most importantly, right now, tens of thousands of families are traumatised, with many millions more feeling, like me, adrift and shocked and hurt. In the next few days, I'll be trying, like many, to figure out what I can do, practically, to help those affected. Maybe I'll even go beyond a T-shirt purchase this time and start getting my shit together with regards to understanding the long term causes of this kind of outrage, and what individual citizens can do to help turn down the heat and minimise the chances of it happening again.

Hopefully.

But I'll tell you what else: I got my Stone Roses tickets, and I got my Download tickets. My leather jacket is in the coat cupboard, but come the summer, it's leaving retirement. And my band is getting back to rehearsals, too.

I'm getting out to some shows. I'm going to reconnect with my tribe.

I'm going back to church.

MY LIFE IN HORROR VOLUME I

Fuck you, fascists.
You don't get to win.

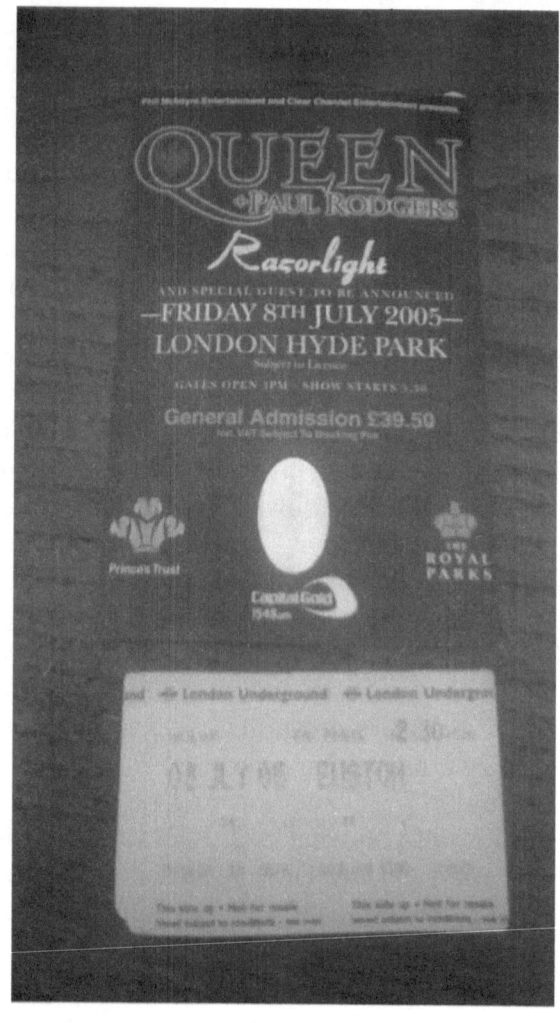

This is *my* faith.

SETTING THE RECORD STRAIGHT:

CLARIFICATIONS

WRITE WHAT SCARES YOU

On Writing

Confession time: The first essay in this book, on *IT,* was, as I mentioned in the introduction, effectively my audition piece for this entire five plus years exercise. In that essay, I made the claim that *IT* was the reason I was a writer. However, while I didn't exactly lie to Jim, I didn't tell the whole truth, either. Yes, I read *IT* when I was eleven; yes, I read it every year for eight or nine years afterwards; yes, I still reread it every three or four years; and yes, it's unquestionably still my favourite Stephen King book, big dumb ending and all.

In that sense, it is absolutely the book that made me. But there's another book, another Stephen King book, in point of fact, without which in all likelihood I would never have penned that article, this one, or any of the stories I've produced in the last five years.

That book is *On Writing*. And I can say, with no exaggeration or hyperbole, that it changed my life.

The book itself is a slender volume. Rereading it for this essay, I was struck again by that—especially when you consider the first third of the book is actually a memoir of sorts (labelled with characteristic King humility as 'C.V.') and the final portion is taken up with the story of the Minivan collision that almost killed him in the summer of

1999. The section of the book actually labelled 'On Writing' is only 40% of the total page count. That's a little deceptive—another 10% is taken up with 'What Writing Is' and a section called 'Toolbox', which is—as you might expect—about the nuts and bolts and mechanics of the craft (and deceptive for another reason which I'll get back to). Still, for a man with a well-earned reputation for verbosity, it's a lethally quick read.

That's utterly deliberate. In the Second Foreword, King opens with the following sentence: 'This is a short book because most books about writing are filled with bullshit.' There's a directness about this statement that resonated strongly with me. I am inherently suspicious of advice about creative pursuits in general and writing in particular. Maybe it's just a prejudice, but I think the best writing (hell, the best creativity) comes from a place of instinct filtered through intellect, not the other way around. 'Write from the heart, edit from the head.' It was thrilling for me to discover that this view was shared by the author of some of my favourite fiction, the writer I would still have to call the single biggest creative influence on me.

This philosophy runs throughout the meat of the book. We learn that King rarely plots, and is even more rarely satisfied when he does (a statement that will come as no shock to some of his critics)—*The Dead Zone* being the only time he was happy with how that worked out. He sees story as a combination of character and situation, something that arises organically as characters come to life and interact with whatever shitstorm has been flung into their lives. A story is a fossil, he tells us, an object found beneath the earth. Your job as a writer is to bring that fossil from the ground gently, a word at a time, discovering its shape as you dig and prod. In this analogy, plotting is a jackhammer—sure, you get something out, but he argues that most of the time you'll shatter the fossil in the process. You'll kill the story.

It's exhilarating, this notion of pulling stories from the earth of the subconscious, of writing as some semi-hypnotic trance. The notion that this was how such towering genre classics as *The Shining*, *Pet Semetary* and *The Stand* were produced was nothing short of staggering. Actually, scratch that, is staggering, present tense. Again, I know critics will snarkily express no surprise at this statement from King, but for me, as a new writer still bleeding his way through his first couple of novels, this is both unsettling and scarily exciting information.

Elsewhere, he offers solid advice about drafting, some thoughts about critical readers and when and how to use them. One especially strong piece of advice, which I stick to fairly hard for the most part, is to place your story in a drawer once you're done, for at least 6-8 weeks, to give yourself distance before coming back for the second swing. He also insists the key to becoming a good writer (assuming a modest baseline of ability) is to read a lot and write a lot, and that there is no shortcut to that.

It is all perfect advice? Of course not. For starters, it was written in 1999, and one or two things have happened in the world of publishing since then. Though I think the advice on how to pursue an agent probably holds up, there's a veritable minefield of options that were not available when this book was written, and in that sense this section is dated. It's a small point, and one that doesn't detract very much from the book overall, but I'd certainly advise that for any brand new writer, in this particular arena, there is a lot of additional reading to be done.

The main thing, though, is just how damn inspirational it is. An entire bank of lights flicked on in my head when I first read King say, 'Do you really need permission to write? Very well, I give you permission.' When he said that all you need to do is take it seriously and do it every day, when he talked about having a railroad spike above the desk where he wrote when he started out, filled with rejection slips—and that's Stephen King!—again, it was revelatory. He wasn't born a world-conquering author—he worked and worked and worked at it. And yes, he had talent, and yes at some point he got lucky, but mainly, he worked and got better. Also... well, also he tells us that he'd do it for free if he had to, and his anecdote substantiates that statement because, for years, he did.

And this is why I wanted to write about this book, outside of the regular *My Life In Horror* format. Because while I could argue almost indefinitely with others about a 'favourite' or 'best' Stephen King book, I am of the firm belief, especially following this reread, that *On Writing* will come to be regarded, rightly, as his most important book. While his fiction will have inspired many into a love of reading, and of genre, I am positive that my experience with *On Writing* is a typical one. I am sure that there's an entire generation of writers working now who are doing so as a direct consequence of picking up this book and being inspired by it, with countless generations still to come that will also do so. I truly believe this book will secure King his greatest and most enduring legacy—hundreds of thousands of storytellers who will take up the pen as a result of *On Writing*.

For a man clearly so in love with the endless thrills and possibilities of storytelling, I can think of no finer achievement. I know for myself that any success I achieve with my writing, modest or huge, will be forever indebted to him, and this book. I will not be alone in this.

Or as King says at the end of the *On Writing* section:

Writing isn't about making money, getting famous, getting dates, getting laid, or making friends. In the end, it's about enriching the lives of those who will read your work, and enriching your life as well. It's about getting up, getting well, and getting over. Getting happy, okay? Getting happy…

…perhaps the best of [this book] *is a permission slip: you can, you should, and if you're brave enough to start, you will. Writing is magic, as much the water of life as any other creative art. The water is free, so drink.*

Drink and be filled up.

Amen, brother.

PS—I mentioned above that claiming that only 50% of the book was the actual 'On Writing' bit was deceptive for a couple of reasons. The second of those reasons, which I only realised on this last read-through, is that both the 'C.V.' chapter and the 'On Living: A Postscript' section (which deals with the Minivan accident) are also, in point of fact, master classes in short form storytelling from a man at the height of his powers. They are so fantastically well written I didn't even notice it the first time; only now, looking back with the benefit of four years of my modest experience at the coalface of prose, do I see just how stunningly well written these sections are. If you haven't recently, I implore you to return to this book and treat yourself—you will immediately see what I mean, I think.

HEY, FUCKERS!

Live: F@*k Like a Suicide

So there's a couple of ways in which this is a swizz—like, for example, I can't claim to have been there when this was first happening. I was seven in 1986. I didn't hear this record until the early summer of 1989, and when I did, it wasn't *this* record—it was the A-Side of the *Lies* album. For that matter, I've never even seen a copy of the original vinyl/cassette release. One of the ways you'll know I've made it as a writer—should ever such an unlikely event come to pass—is that I will buy this sucker on vinyl and play it loud enough to break windows.

So, on the one hand, there's a way in which I can't talk about what this was like when it came out. On the other hand, only about ten thousand people plausibly can, given it was a limited edition pressing. Considering the seismic effect the band were about to have, though, and further given that the recording, if not the format, was given a general release, it feels worth talking about. And also, in fairness to me, when I did hear this record, it changed my life, as I discussed in the opening section of this book.

And you know what? It's still completely fucking awesome. In fact, as much as *Appetite For Destruction* is in my all-time top five, I think there's a serious case to be made that GnR never sounded better than they do on *Live Like A Suicide*.

In fact, fuck it; I've had a drink. Let's make that case.

A good EP will always beat a good album; let's start there. The reason is obvious; it's a numbers game. Writing a genuinely classic album—eight, ten, even twelve tracks, all killer no filler, as the kids say, is a tough assignment. It's normally just about possible for a debut—because most debut albums represent anywhere from five to ten years of work, with only the best songs from that period making it to the top—but even then, it's almost impossible to maintain a level of absolute top drawer quality. I mean, I love 'Anything Goes', but I can't argue that it's as essential a song as 'Welcome To The Jungle'.

A four track EP, however, is a different proposition. You don't have to worry so much about ebb and flow, track sequencing, where to put the ballad. Instead, you can simply open the can of whoop-ass and splode it out onto the plate in one go. Do it right, and you'll produce a fifteen-minute espresso shot of sound so raw and exciting the immediate response of your listener will simply be to flip that sucker back over and drop the needle again.

'Live Like A Suicide' serves as an exemplar of this form.

After the raw statement of intent that is Slash yelling 'Hey! Fuckers! Fucking Guns and fucking Roses!' over a howling stadium crowd, 'Reckless Life' just explodes into being, a machine gun snare roll leading into a dirty, furious guitar riff. It begs to be played loud, to be let off the leash and shown what it can do, and if you acquiesce, it will reward your ringing eardrums with a ferocity and rage that burns in your brain. The drumming is relentless, the guitars in perfect sync, and oh my lord that vocal. Axl may be one of the most unpleasant ego trippers in a field with some stiff competition, but that boy has pipes. And here, with those vocals matched perfectly to the melody and lyric, it's nothing short of intoxicating. They may have looked like just another hair metal band, but there's as much punk here as there is classic rock. It's dirty, exhilarating, aggressive, and raw.

It's also three minutes long. Wham bam.

'Nice Boys', the first of two covers, takes a Rose Tattoo classic, and has The Dammed play it at 1000 miles an hour, with a vocal better than the Angry Anderson original (sorry, but it's true). Again, the rhythm section is tremendous, the drumming off the hook, the bass runs in the drop out chorus perfect, and those guitars! I know everyone goes on about Slash, and I'm not saying he doesn't deserve it, but for my money Izzy Stradlin may be the most underrated rhythm guitarist of his generation. Sure, there's a lot of open chord work in the verses, but listen close to the little flourishes he puts into them, or his note perfect support in the intro of the following track, and fucking marvel, kids. They don't make 'em like that any more. Also, it's a perfect choice of cover for this group—when Axl sneers 'I bet your mama said, Nice Boys! Don't play rock 'n *roll*!' you can hear the knicker elastic snapping at 6000 miles and thirty-five years remove.

After a quick fade out/in, next up is 'Move To The City'—twin guitar intro, snare roll, into a swaggering, horn-inflected groove. This one comes on like *Pump* era Aerosmith in a lot of ways, but again, there's that punk edge to the guitars and vocals that give it just a few more teeth in the grin. The run up at the end of the guitar solo, back into the bridge, is a thing of beauty. Axl's 'small town white boy' roots are on proud display in the lyric (a tendency that would reach its ugly peak in the still-shocking 'One In A Million'), that snarling misogyny that fuels so much of the fury of *Appetite*... already making itself known, not-quite-hidden behind a wry grin.

Speaking of casual misogyny, 'This is a song about your fucking mother,' introduces the final cover, a blistering run through Aerosmith's '73 classic 'Mama Kin'. Again, GnR add grit and spit to a classic rock anthem, giving it a raw vitality that belies the age of the song. The guitars take it in turns to play the single verse lick under the vocal, and again, I couldn't tell you which was Izzy and which Slash (well, okay, I could, but I've listened to it, like, a million times). It's faultless execution, displaying just how tight a unit the band was. Punk energy allied to classic rock skills, a soon-to-be-world-conquering combination.

And by the way, it's fake. I mean, I realise I'm probably the last person in the world to learn this, but it's not actually a live recording. I remember when I sat to research this article thinking that the recordings must have been done as part of the stadium tour they did with Aerosmith. I couldn't figure out where else they'd have that kind of a crowd noise behind them. But of course, in 1986, GnR was still two years out from hitting the road as the opening act for the

HEY, FUCKERS!

Permanent Vacation Tour. In '86, they were lucky to fill a bar.

So they did the only honourable thing—they cheated. They recorded the four tracks live in the studio, then piped in the crowd noise from some Texas stadium rock show.

So it turns out one of my favourite live recording of all times… isn't.

But you know what? I couldn't care less. I've had the pleasure of listening to this EP on repeat while I've been writing this, and I'm here to tell you, friends and neighbours, it holds up fine. There was something special about GnR, something that elevated them above the LA Glam/Hair metal circus they came screaming out of. Sure, some of those other bands had that punk/New York Dolls influence, and sure, some had that Aerosmith/classic rock thing going on too. But nobody melded those traditions as perfectly. GnR took the raw classic rock elements of melody, songwriting and technical ability, and welded them to the ferocity, pace, and DIY fuck-you of punk. In so doing, they created a machine that, while not suited to long-term stability, would nonetheless make a noise loud enough to, briefly, surmount the world.

And it's never sounded clearer, dirtier, rawer, or more urgent than it does on *Live Like A Suicide*. All the pieces are here—the musicianship, the aggression, the hunger.

Most of all, the hunger.

In fact, yeah, it's true. They never sounded better.

END OF SIDE ONE

I HAPPEN TO BE CRAZY. NOT STUPID.

A Death in the Family

Author's note: The essay below was written on 3rd November 2016, before the US presidential election result was known. I have never been less happy that my gut was right. I have never been more afraid for the future than I am now. Please be kind to each other. The world is going to need a lot of that in the months and years ahead, I suspect.
The bastards locked the door.
K

In a final analysis, I got it because it was cheap.

I am somewhere around the twelve/thirteen mark, to the best of my recollection. Thirteen, tops. Old enough that my dad had allowed me to read *The Dark Knight Returns*, I think—a seminal experience for any Batman fan. And I almost certainly picked it up during one of my occasional weekend pilgrimages to that thriving hub of commerce, Exeter, and specifically the Dillons in the city centre (a business that, at the time of writing, has morphed into a Waterstones, and is still present, in the same big building on the same street corner as it was in my childhood).

I will have wanted More. More Batman. More comic book goodness.

And the sad truth was that most comic books, most trade collections anyway, were expensive. The huge *Batman Vs The Joker: The Greatest Joker Stories Ever Told*, for example, would have been at least £8.99, maybe more. I did eventually pick that sucker up when it was on sale, but no way was I paying full sticker price, with £20 a month being my allowance, and the bus journey alone swallowing £5 of that. Not with music to buy as well. I mean, I loved comics and books, but let's not go crazy.

So this will have sung to me, I suspect. Lovely black cover. Ominous art. The back cover, recreating the covers of the original four-issue comic run, alongside some truly hyperbolic press quotes. And of course, most importantly, that lovely £2.50 price sticker.

Sold. *Death In The Family* was coming home with me.

I've popped the name, because I want to give y'all a chance to back out now. It may sound stupid, talking spoilers about a comic that came out in '89, before some of you were born. But this is, in my opinion, one of The Big Ones—as classic and defining as *Dark Knight*, *Watchmen*, *Transmetropolitan*. Yeah, I'm serious. So in the unlikely event you haven't read it, and don't understand its cultural significance, back the hell away from the article, and go and spend £2.50 in today's money on the collection, okay?

Thank me later.

Back? Good.

I read it on the bus on the way home. All of it. The

I HAPPEN TO BE CRAZY. NOT STUPID.

totally weird, po-faced introduction, where some Dr. from the future rattled on about the 'unique 20th century pathology of the costumed superhero' or whatever, through to the still-a-bit-defensive postscript from Dennis O'Neil, featuring the heart stopping final vote tally—holy shit, this was a close one.

I mean, I poured over it. Obsessed. I remember reading it over and over and over again, in the weeks, months and years that followed. I even, God help me, tried to sketch a couple of the panels from the comic—a full face shot of Batman from the last issue, from his interrogation with the CIA guy, and another of the Joker at the UN in the Iranian headdress. Not trace, you understand, but draw, freehand—I was trying to recreate the pictures as faithfully as I could, trying to get my clumsy hand to push the pencil over the page as the artist had done.

Trying to understand the magic. Trying to feel it.

I have a recollection of also trying to turn it into a radio play, roping in friends to play the other parts, using the in-built microphone in my sister's cassette recorder. I mean, I was nuts about this damn story. The contours of the narrative, and many of the individual art panels, are seared into my brain, scarring it as surely as acid scarred Harvey Dent in the courtroom.

I mean, fucking hell, this story.

The setup is great. Say what you like about DC in the late 80s, they knew how to do melodrama. Having Jason Todd, Robin number two, going increasingly off the rails, still not dealing with the death of his parents, tracks well, and adds a nice early helping of guilt for Bruce as he contemplates the wisdom of his masked-vigilantism-as-grief-therapy approach to sidekick recruitment. The section where Batman (the narrator for the story) hypothesizes about where Jason's angry walk will take him shouldn't work… but it does. And the moment where Jason discovers, via a water damaged birth certificate, that the woman he thought was his mother wasn't is a genuine spine tingler. These are the fundamental pillars of the Batman mythos, after all; vigilante equals orphan. The discovery that Jason may not in fact be a paid up member of the Dead Parents Club puts his status as Robin in jeopardy, in a way Bruce's 'temporary suspension' never did. Likewise, his decision to go after his mother solo makes sense—or at least as much sense as teenagers ever make.

Meanwhile, as a newspaper headline informs us, The Joker Escapes Again.

He's just fucking brilliant in this. Smart, capricious, vicious, cunning, desperate, and utterly, violently insane. The story takes place just after *The Killing Joke* (indeed, there's references to 'What He Did To Barbara' that flew over my head until years later), so the conceit that the Joker is having to sell his cruise missile with a nuclear warhead to raise funds makes sense—even if his hints, in chapter one, that he's looking to get into the international diplomacy game feel a touch odd. But mainly, it's just My Joker, the one who never made it fully to screen until Heath Ledger—the guy who is a rampant cancer cell, tearing through humanity with a blood soaked grin, leaving a trail of bodies.

I HAPPEN TO BE CRAZY. NOT STUPID.

He's not even very funny.

I remember being utterly gripped by his sociopathy, his casual cruelty. The fact that Robin's possible candidates for mother (the three women who shared the first initial with the birth certificate and were also in his father's address book) were all based in the middle east, the same place Joker and his bomb were heading, feels laughably contrived now, but felt reasonable then. Mainly, I suspect, because a combination of sheer pace—aside from the recaps at the start of each chapter the story zips along pretty well—and also a feeling of inevitability. This is, after all, a tragedy, and tragedy has its own shape and pace and weight.

And it really does feel bad. There's a menace that hangs over the first two books—especially the second, when in true thriller fashion, we know long before Jason that the Joker is blackmailing his mother. I can still remember the relief when Jason went back to get Batman, telling him the Joker had taken his mother—and then the dread I felt as they realised the booby-trapped supplies were already in convoy, and Batman was going to have to leave Jason to watch the warehouse while he went after the lorries. The scene is brilliant—Batman, hands on Jason's shoulders, pleading with him to wait, to not take the Joker on, while Jason stands, stony-faced. Promising he will.

Batman doesn't believe him. But he goes anyway. He has to.

We see Jason's thoughts as the BatCopter lifts off and he shields his eyes from the swirling desert sands. We know he's going into the warehouse. It's a sickening sinking feeling. I get it every single time I read the story. Every time.

He goes down to the warehouse. Reveals his secret to his mother. She invites him inside.

She turns him over to the Joker.

It's horrible. She pulls a gun, her beautiful face suddenly hard, as she explains she's been dipping into the funds, that any Bat interference will uncover her crimes as well as the Jokers's. His birth mother betrays him, hours after he meets her for the first time. Delivered into the custody of his mentors' most dangerous opponent.

The Joker beats him. He feigns unconsciousness, then fights back. Two of the Joker's enormous goons knock him to the floor, one kicking him in the ribs. He balls up, clearly in agony.

The Joker picks up a crowbar, and beats the shit out of him.

We see the first blow land across his back, and what might be spit or blood spew out of his mouth. Then a series of panels of the Joker, bring the crowbar down. Again. And Again. And Again. He's sweating, mouth not just grinning but gaping. The end of the crowbar becomes bloody. Jason's mother watches, then turns away in disgust, and lights a cigarette.

By the time Joker is done, his gloves are also stained red. We see only a bloodied leg of the Boy Wonder on the edge of the panel. As the Joker recovers from his frenzy, and realises what terrible danger he's put himself in, he leaves Jason's mother tied up in the warehouse, with a bomb timed to explode.

I HAPPEN TO BE CRAZY. NOT STUPID.

I mean, I can't even. The sadism of it would often bring out prickly fear sweats in me as I read it. This was something taboo, verbotten. The bad guys were bad, sure, innocent people would get hurt, even killed, shit, that happened even in *Doctor Who*… but this was Robin. This was a kid. Not just a kid, but also Batman's sidekick. This. Did. Not. Happen.

And it was happening.

It went on happening, as the panel pattern showed the timer counting down, alongside widescreen shots of the warehouse. As, around the two minute mark, Robin regained consciousness, with a ruined face not unlike that of a certain recent *Walking Dead* cast member, as I think about it, and crawled first to the device, then, realising he was in no fit state to handle it, to his mother.

There's a little under a minute to go as he unties the rope and collapses, urging her to leave. Around forty seconds by the time she's got an arm over his shoulders and has pulled him up. They stagger to the door, painfully slow, as the clock ticks-ticks-ticks.

They reach the door with ten seconds to spare.

And it's locked.

The last panel inside the warehouse is a close up of Jason's mother, her eyes wide and pupils dilated with terror. 'The Joker locked the door!'

Kahboom.

We see the Batman's face lit by the fireball, then the last panel is behind him, as he walks towards the smoking wreckage. 'Jason… no…'

Some fucking writer. I just cannot put into words what that did to me. What it *does* to me. It's the locked door, I think. We've seen this scene before, after all. Just a few times. The last minute escape from the big boom. But that fucking locked door. It's like the Joker has seen the same movies we have seen, and decided, 'Not this time, baby!' It's a classic moment of pure sadistic villainy—a final twist of the knife delivered by an expert in inflicting misery, suffering and death.

Even more than *The Killing Joke*, this was the moment, for me, that the Joker cemented his position as Batman's archnemesis, for all time. No matter the wealth, powers, or intelligence of the rest of the rogues gallery, no one was *ever* going to top this moment.

Infamy.

Interesting to note, therefore, that there were two possible Batman 428's written—one where Jason lived, one where he died. I speculated furiously about that, as a kid, trying to envisage what that other issue might look like, how the scenario might play out (the version of events I eventually hit on was that in the other comic, his mother shields Jason from the blast. She is killed, thereby keeping 'A Death In The Family' and Jason is hospitalised, leaving the Bat to go after Joker alone—and no, I have no idea, but I bet it was something like that). I know intellectually that it was a phone vote that decided Jason's fate, and that the final tally from over 10,000 calls was damnably close, with less than 100 votes separating the result (sad to say, I still find this one of the most compelling arguments for voting in general—you never know when it's going to be close, as recent events have proven). Yet, for all that, the ending we got feels utterly inevitable.

I HAPPEN TO BE CRAZY. NOT STUPID.

And, you know, it's far from the last time a popular vote has left me sick to my stomach, with both the closeness of the result and the wrongness of the outcome—the feeling like reality has swung a curveball, that we've fallen away from some theoretical future line of best fit and been cast into some crappy alternate reality where Picard is a bad guy and the Brigadier wears an eyepatch. As I write this, we're a week out from a US presidential election where a badly written Batman villain has a non-trivial chance of becoming the leader of the free world, and by the time you read this, you'll know if we dodged that bullet, and if so, how closely by.

But right now, I don't know if we dodged it at all. I don't know if we made it out the door in time. I don't know if the bomb went off.

I don't know if hope lies, bleeding and battered but still breathing, or if it's been shredded utterly by the blast. But I am starting to get a terrible feeling—that sickening, sinking sense of inevitability. Tragedy has a pattern, after all. It has a shape and a rhythm and a pace. I've rarely wanted more fervently to be wrong.

A Death In The Family is still a scary story.

We still live in a very scary world.

WHAT HAVE WE LEARNED?

An Afterword

It's quite a trip, to go back over three years of your own writing.

My Life In Horror is a project I'd always envisaged as having a limited run—and indeed, as I write this, the plan is for eight more posts to round things out to an even sixty. It's an arbitrary figure, but it feels expansive enough to cover the high and low points without, hopefully, outstaying its welcome; after all, how many times can you claim to have experienced something seminal or life changing before those words lose meaning?

And yet, one thing that's come back at me forcibly as I read through and revise those first thirty essays for this edition is just how blessed my life has been by some truly tremendous art; especially in those earliest years. Related to that, another observation: just how much of that art was consumed at wildly unsuitable ages.

And that's still giving me pause. Because as I came to rearrange these essays in the order I encountered them (as opposed to the authored order, which was almost always 'what the fuck am I going to write about this month?'), I found myself boggled by some of the encounters. *Temple Of Doom* at seven? Single digits for Carpenter's *The Thing*? For

WHAT HAVE WE LEARNED?

that matter, what are we to make of the fact that a version of *War Of The Worlds* is one of my earliest memories of narrative full stop?

No wonder I turned out as I did. I blame the parents.

Only here's the thing, not only am I not alone on this, I'm beginning to suspect this experience is near-as-dammit universal. Certainly, in the many conversations I have been fortunate to have with fellow creatives in the horror field, there's always some hilariously unsuitable work lurking at a ludicrously young age, the troll under the bridge of imagination.

We joke, uneasily, about damage and scarring, psychological trauma, har-har, before turning the conversation to our efforts to scare current and future generations.

And that could get uneasy, very quickly indeed, but for one simple, intractable fact; I wouldn't trade it for anything. Every single essay in this book represents an experience I hold dear. Whether joy, pain, or some uneasy cocktail, these essays represent significant waypoints on my journey to becoming… whatever the hell I'm still in the process of becoming. I mean, dead, obviously, eventually, but before that hopefully other things.

And I think—*I think*—my tentative, subject-to-revision thesis, gleaned from all this psychological excavation, is that human life basically *is* a horror show, what with arbitrary, unjust suffering, political systems that place unimaginable power into the hands of sociopaths (for whom, to paraphrase Henry Rollins, we are all ants whose flesh tastes like chicken), and worst of all, the ability to imagine and truly comprehend the fact of our mortality without having anything but the faintest and most illusory control over it.

Given that, even as we attempt to comprehend the horror, we must also seek and find joy. Increasingly I believe that doing so is both a moral imperative and an act of profound rebellion against both the cruelty of some of our fellow humans, and the cold indifference of the wider universe.

And to, at least sometimes, be able to find that joy, that catharsis, *within* the horror itself… ah, that's the kind of mad alchemy that gives me hope for our collective future. Writing in 2020, that feels about as far from frivolous as it's possible to get—in fact, I'd go so far as to call it an essential tool for psychological survival.

May we all be blessed with such tools, as we face what is to come.

And should this book have pointed you towards one or two such signposts—or even serve as just a glimpse of how such alchemy may, sometimes, be performed—well, I consider that time well spent indeed.

KP 13/01/2020

Acknowledgements

In addition to the people thanked in the dedication and special thanks, I must thank Ray Cluley, Tracy Fahey, Chris Hall, JR Park, Johnny Mains, Tim Major, Alasdair Stuart, John Llewellyn Probert and Neil Snowdon, all of whom read an early copy of the text and provided feedback and support. I'm deeply honoured to have so many dear and talented friends in the writing community, and without their support for this project, it's unlikely it would have seen the light of day. And that goes double to everyone who backed the crowdfunder. Thank you for supporting this mad project. I hope you have as much fun reading it as I did writing it.

Rowan B. Fortune, of Rowan Tree Editing (www.rowantree-editing.uk) completed the structural and line edit with speed, thoroughness, and attention to detail. His work was invaluable in improving the readability of the manuscript. Much thanks.

Steve Shaw of WHITEspace (www.white-space.uk) took care of the typesetting, formatting, and cover design for all editions of the book, in the process boiling my crazed half-witterings down to book covers so good, you could be forgiven for thinking I knew what I was doing (I didn't).

And Matt Dovey (www.mattdovey.com) designed the logo and promotional materials for the crowdfunding campaign. I can recommend working with all three unreservedly.

Feels superfluous to thank Jim again, but what the

hell? Thanks for your faith in my writing. It meant, and continues to mean, the world. Gingernuts4Life!

And last, and in many ways most, thanks as ever to my wife and children, who continue to support my hacking away at the keyboard, in search of... something or other. You are my favourite story, and my happily ever after.

www.ingramcontent.com/pod-product-compliance
Lightning Source LLC
Chambersburg PA
CBHW020857110526
R18273100001B/R182731PG44587CBX00001B/1